JAY-Z

HIP-HOP ICON

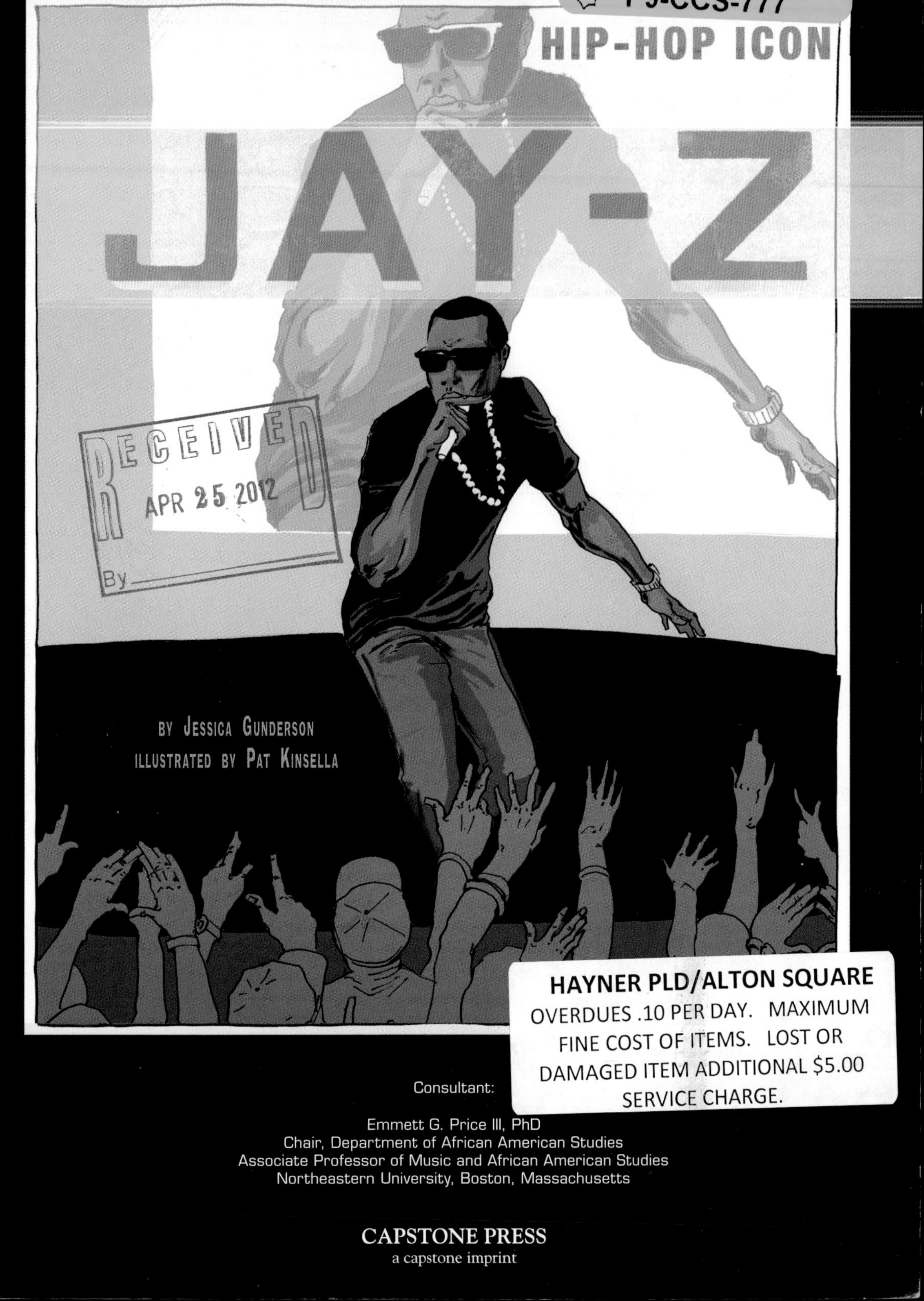

BY JESSICA GUNDERSON
ILLUSTRATED BY PAT KINSELLA

Consultant:

Emmett G. Price III, PhD
Chair, Department of African American Studies
Associate Professor of Music and African American Studies
Northeastern University, Boston, Massachusetts

CAPSTONE PRESS
a capstone imprint

Graphic Library is published by Capstone Press,
1710 Roe Crest Drive
North Mankato, Minnesota 56003
www.capstonepub.com

Books published by Capstone Press are
manufactured with paper containing at least
10 percent post-consumer waste.

Library of Congress Cataloging-in-Publication Data
Gunderson, Jessica.
  Jay-Z : hip-hop icon / by Jessica Gunderson.
    p. cm. — (Graphic library. American graphic)
  Includes bibliographical references and index.
  Summary: "In graphic novel format, describes the
life of Jay-Z focusing on his music career and business
success"—Provided by publisher.
  ISBN 978-1-4296-6017-4 (library binding)
  ISBN 978-1-4296-7993-0 (paperback)
  1. Jay-Z, 1969—Juvenile literature. 2. Rap musicians—
United States—Biography—Juvenile literature. I. Title.
  ML3930.J38G86 2012
  782.421649092—dc23 [B]   2011034042

Direct quotes appear on the following pages in orange:

5, 18, 21, from *Fade to Black* directed by Pat Paulson and Michael
John Warren (Hollywood: Paramount Classics, 2004)

7, from *Decoded* by Jay-Z (New York: Spiegel & Grau, 2010)

15, from "Jay-Z Plans Grammy Boycott," MTV, February 24, 1999
(www.mtv.com/)

17, from "Jay-Z Returns," Entertainment Weekly, September 15,
2006 (www.ew.com/)

22, from "Jay-Z Named President of Def Jam Records," USA
Today, December 8, 2004 (www.usatoday.com)

28, from "The J to Z of Jay-Z: The Making of a Hip-Hop
Heavyweight," MTV, August 20, 2009 (www.mtv.com/)

Photo Credit: Corbis: Rune Hellestad, 29

Art Director: Nathan Gassman
Editor: Mari Bolte
Production Specialist: Laura Manthe

Printed in the United States of America in Stevens Point, Wisconsin.
102011   006404WZS12

Chapter 1 SOLD OUT

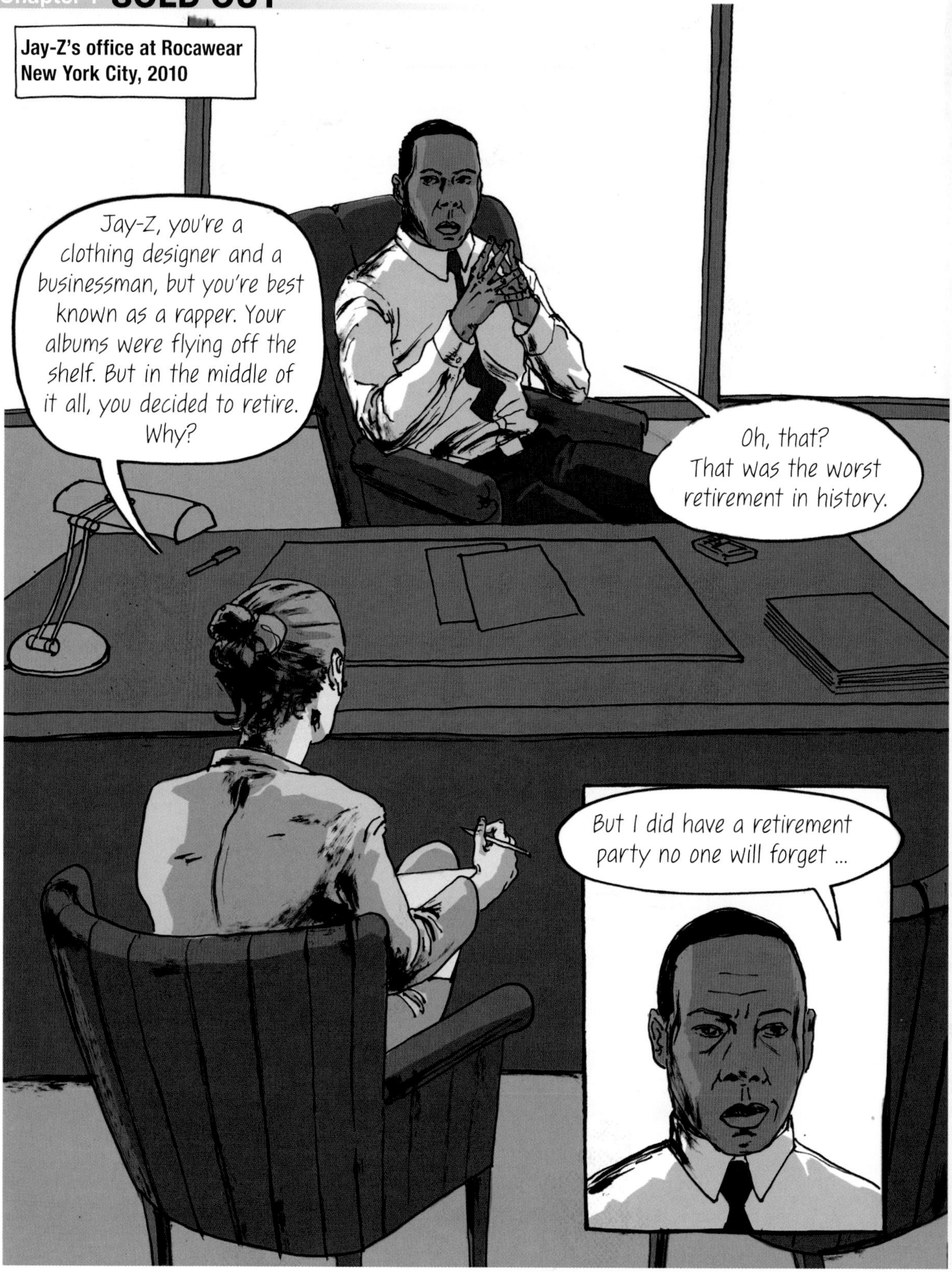
Jay-Z's office at Rocawear
New York City, 2010
Jay-Z, you're a clothing designer and a businessman, but you're best known as a rapper. Your albums were flying off the shelf. But in the middle of it all, you decided to retire. Why?
Oh, that? That was the worst retirement in history.
But I did have a retirement party no one will forget ...

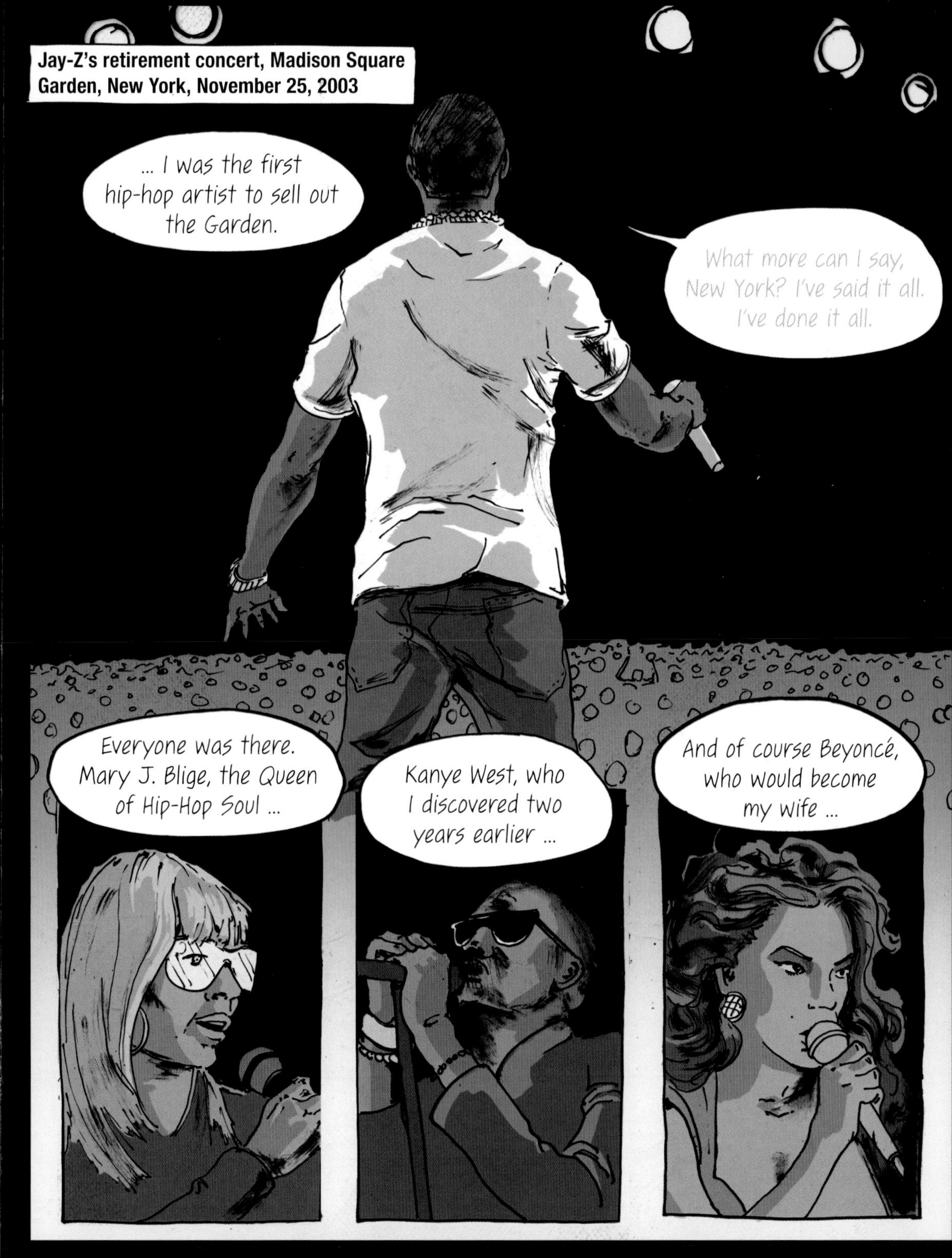
Jay-Z's retirement concert, Madison Square Garden, New York, November 25, 2003
... I was the first hip-hop artist to sell out the Garden.
What more can I say, New York? I've said it all. I've done it all.
Everyone was there. Mary J. Blige, the Queen of Hip-Hop Soul ...
Kanye West, who I discovered two years earlier ...
And of course Beyoncé, who would become my wife ...

Chapter 2 A HARD-KNOCK LIFE

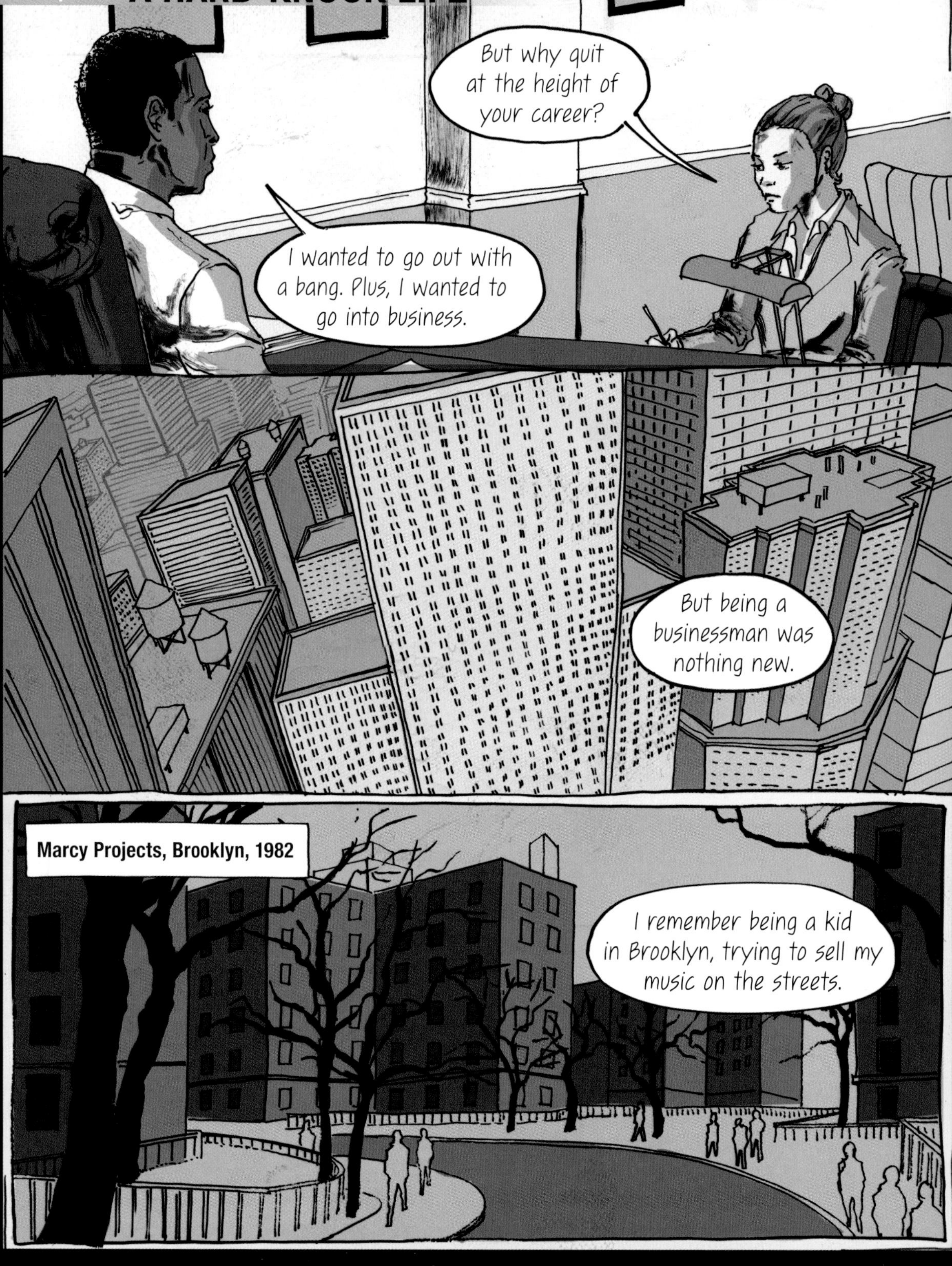
But why quit at the height of your career?
I wanted to go out with a bang. Plus, I wanted to go into business.
But being a businessman was nothing new.
Marcy Projects, Brooklyn, 1982
I remember being a kid in Brooklyn, trying to sell my music on the streets.

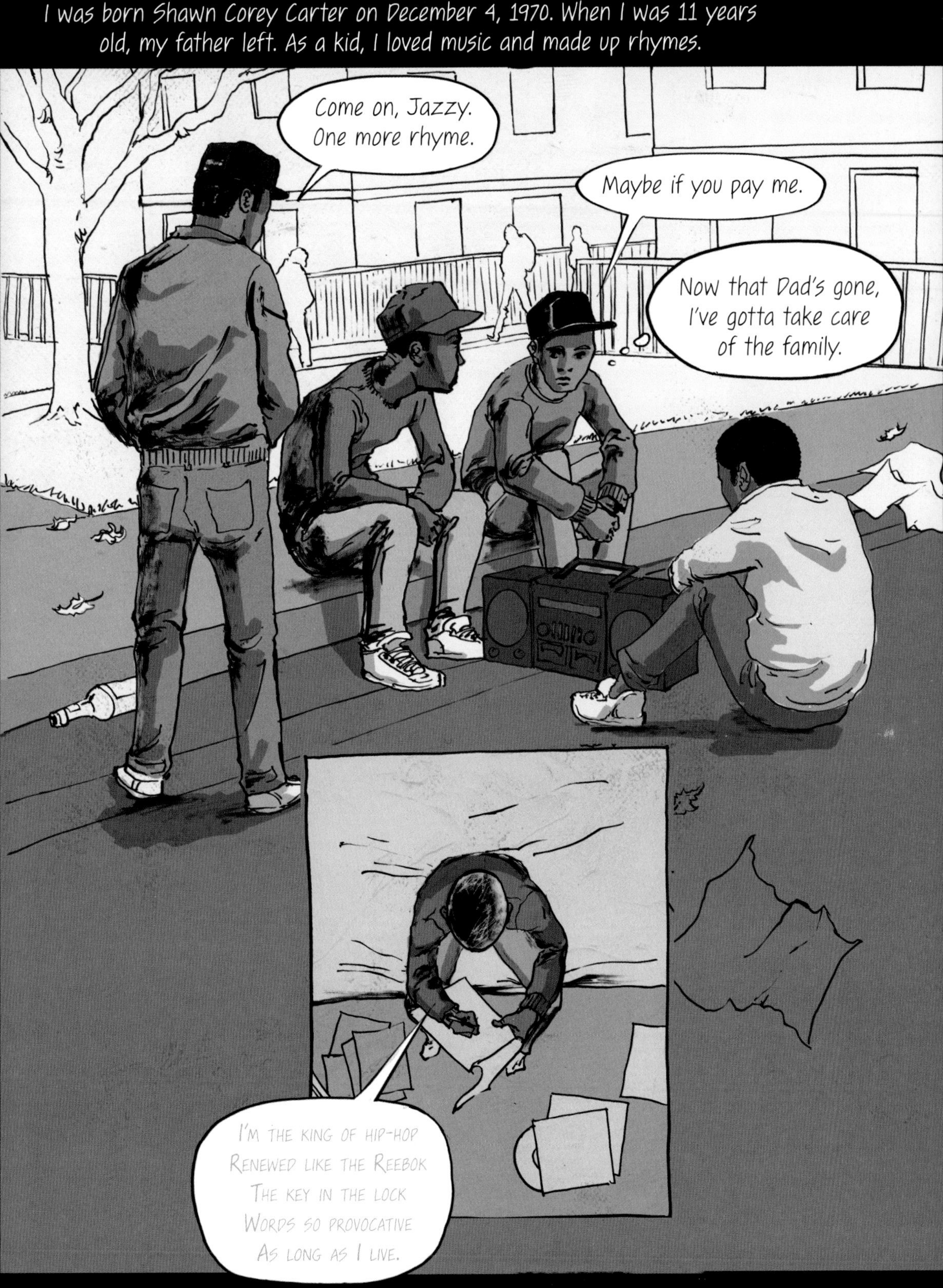
I was born Shawn Corey Carter on December 4, 1970. When I was 11 years old, my father left. As a kid, I loved music and made up rhymes.
Come on, Jazzy. One more rhyme.
Maybe if you pay me.
Now that Dad's gone, I've gotta take care of the family.
I'M THE KING OF HIP-HOP
RENEWED LIKE THE REEBOK
THE KEY IN THE LOCK
WORDS SO PROVOCATIVE
AS LONG AS I LIVE.

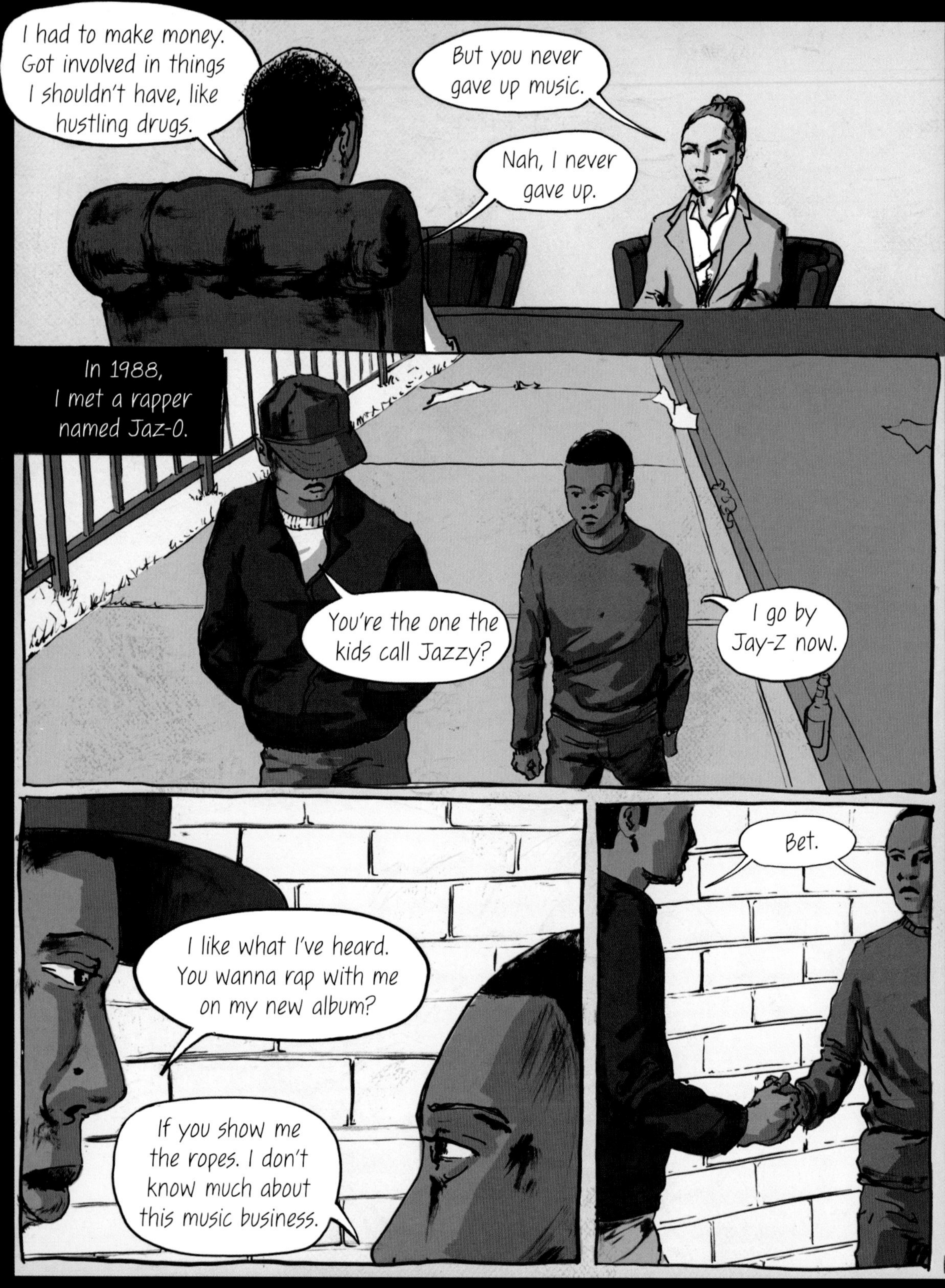
I had to make money. Got involved in things I shouldn't have, like hustling drugs.
But you never gave up music.
Nah, I never gave up.
In 1988, I met a rapper named Jaz-O.
You're the one the kids call Jazzy?
I go by Jay-Z now.
I like what I've heard. You wanna rap with me on my new album?
If you show me the ropes. I don't know much about this music business.
Bet.

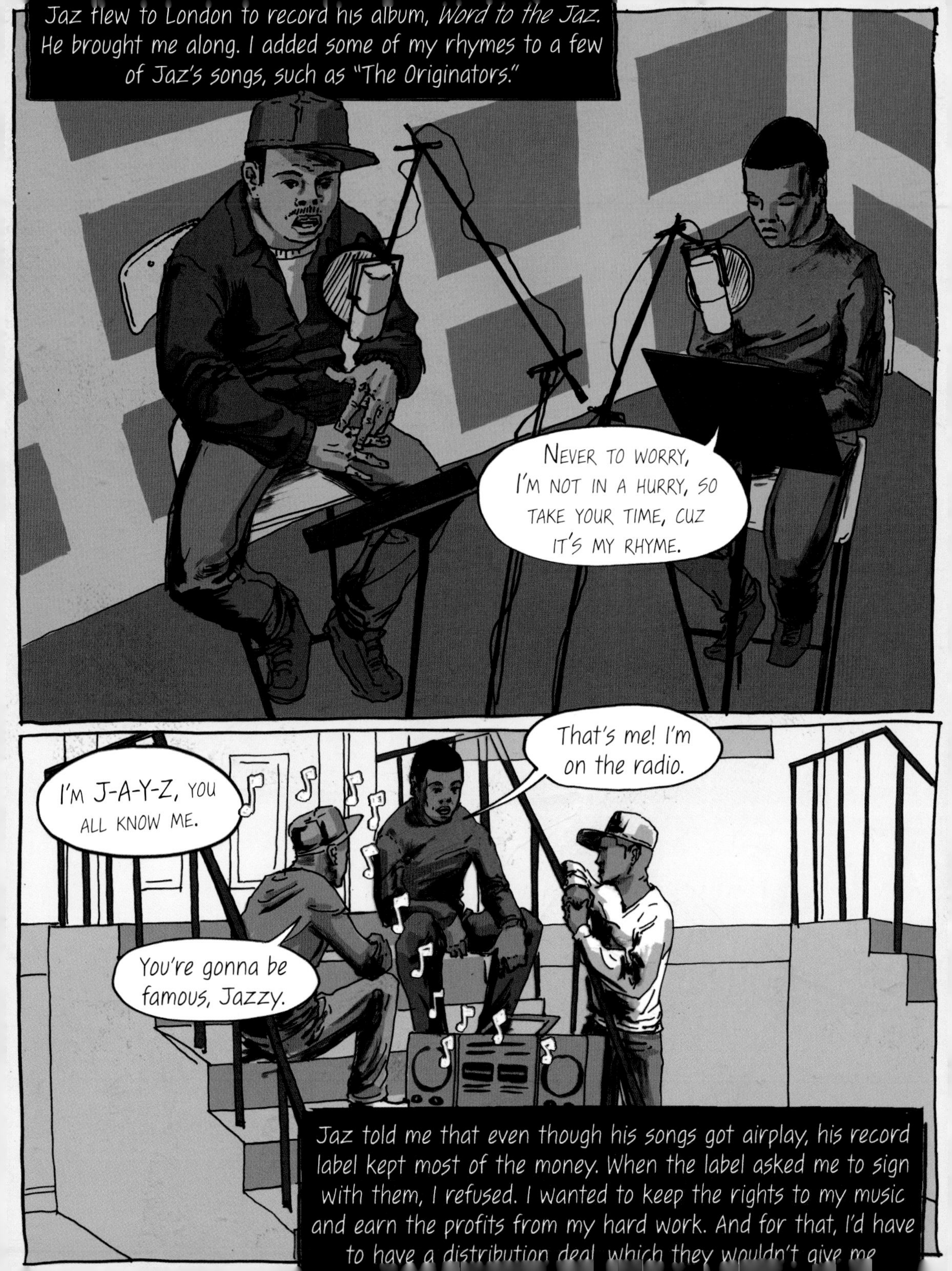
Jaz flew to London to record his album, *Word to the Jaz.* He brought me along. I added some of my rhymes to a few of Jaz's songs, such as "The Originators."
NEVER TO WORRY, I'M NOT IN A HURRY, SO TAKE YOUR TIME, CUZ IT'S MY RHYME.
I'M J-A-Y-Z, YOU ALL KNOW ME.
That's me! I'm on the radio.
You're gonna be famous, Jazzy.
Jaz told me that even though his songs got airplay, his record label kept most of the money. When the label asked me to sign with them, I refused. I wanted to keep the rights to my music and earn the profits from my hard work. And for that, I'd have to have a distribution deal, which they wouldn't give me

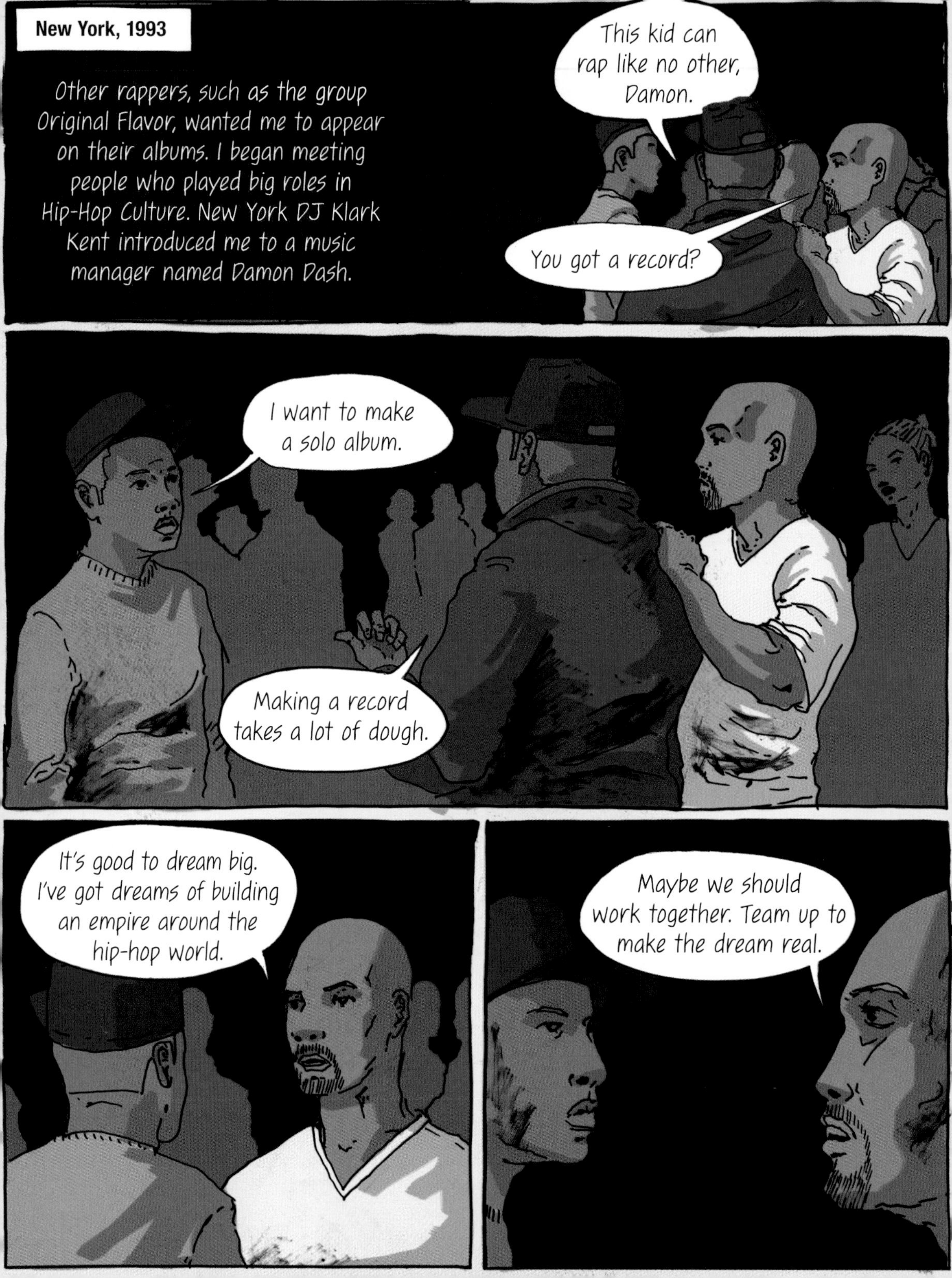
New York, 1993
Other rappers, such as the group Original Flavor, wanted me to appear on their albums. I began meeting people who played big roles in Hip-Hop Culture. New York DJ Klark Kent introduced me to a music manager named Damon Dash.
This kid can rap like no other, Damon.
You got a record?
I want to make a solo album.
Making a record takes a lot of dough.
It's good to dream big. I've got dreams of building an empire around the hip-hop world.
Maybe we should work together. Team up to make the dream real.

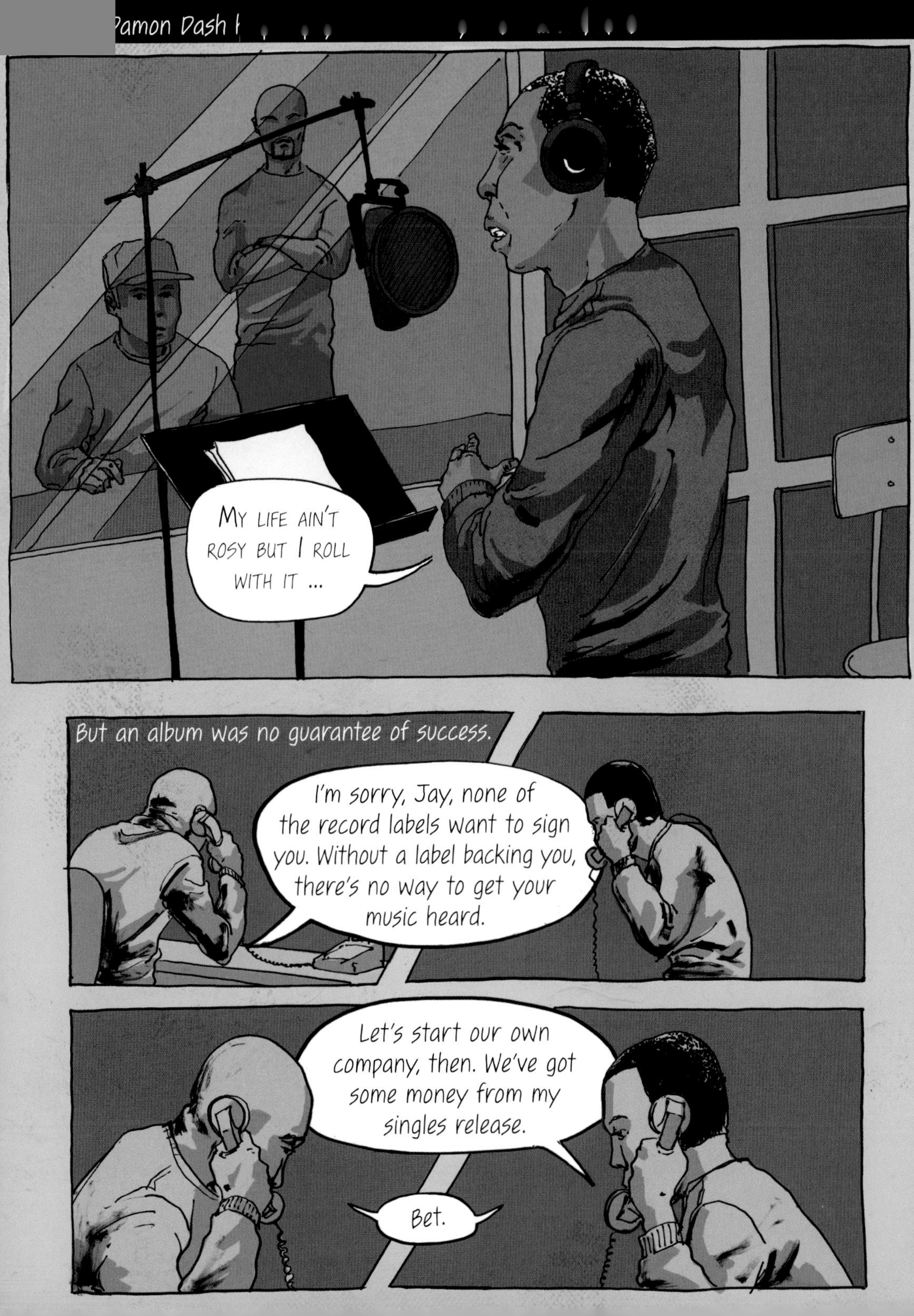
Damon Dash [redacted]
My life ain't rosy but I roll with it ...
But an album was no guarantee of success.
I'm sorry, Jay, none of the record labels want to sign you. Without a label backing you, there's no way to get your music heard.
Let's start our own company, then. We've got some money from my singles release.
Bet.

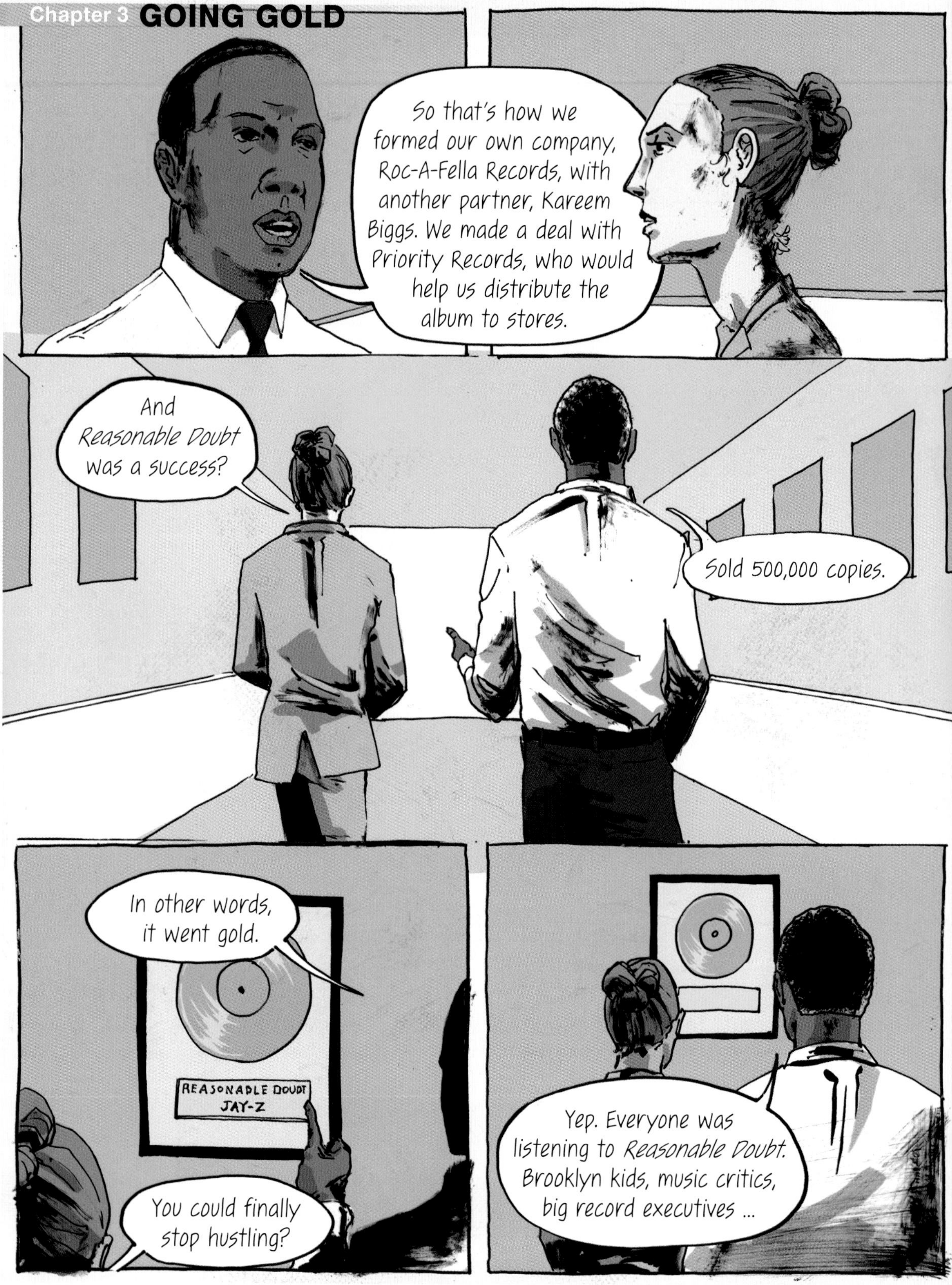
So that's how we formed our own company, Roc-A-Fella Records, with another partner, Kareem Biggs. We made a deal with Priority Records, who would help us distribute the album to stores.
And *Reasonable Doubt* was a success?
Sold 500,000 copies.
In other words, it went gold.
REASONABLE DOUBT JAY-Z
You could finally stop hustling?
Yep. Everyone was listening to *Reasonable Doubt*. Brooklyn kids, music critics, big record executives ...

After *Reasonable Doubt*'s release in 1996, Def Jam Records, one of the greatest labels in the hip-hop world, contacted Roc-A-Fella.

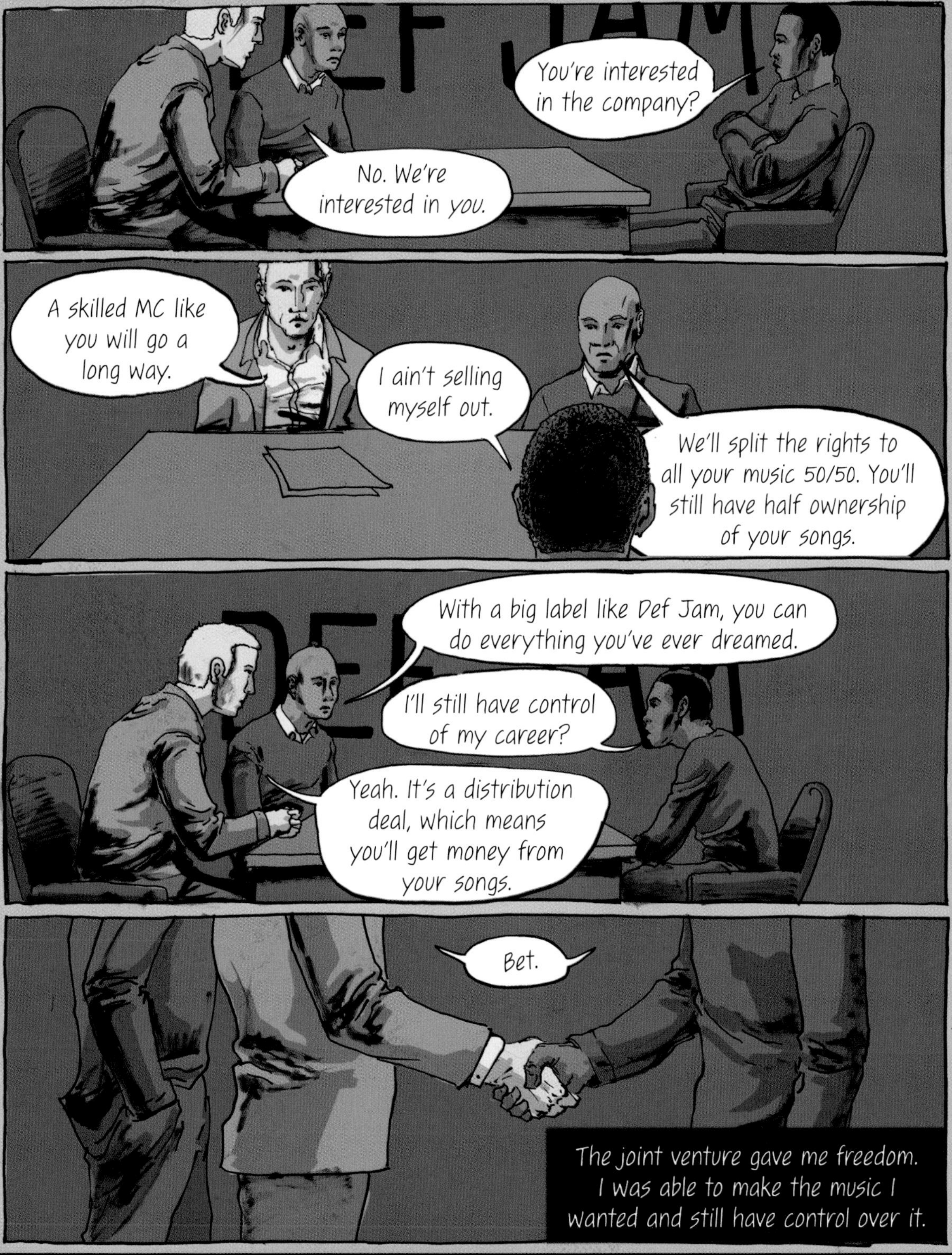

DEF JAM
You're interested in the company?
No. We're interested in *you*.
A skilled MC like you will go a long way.
I ain't selling myself out.
We'll split the rights to all your music 50/50. You'll still have half ownership of your songs.
With a big label like Def Jam, you can do everything you've ever dreamed.
I'll still have control of my career?
Yeah. It's a distribution deal, which means you'll get money from your songs.
Bet.
The joint venture gave me freedom. I was able to make the music I wanted and still have control over it.

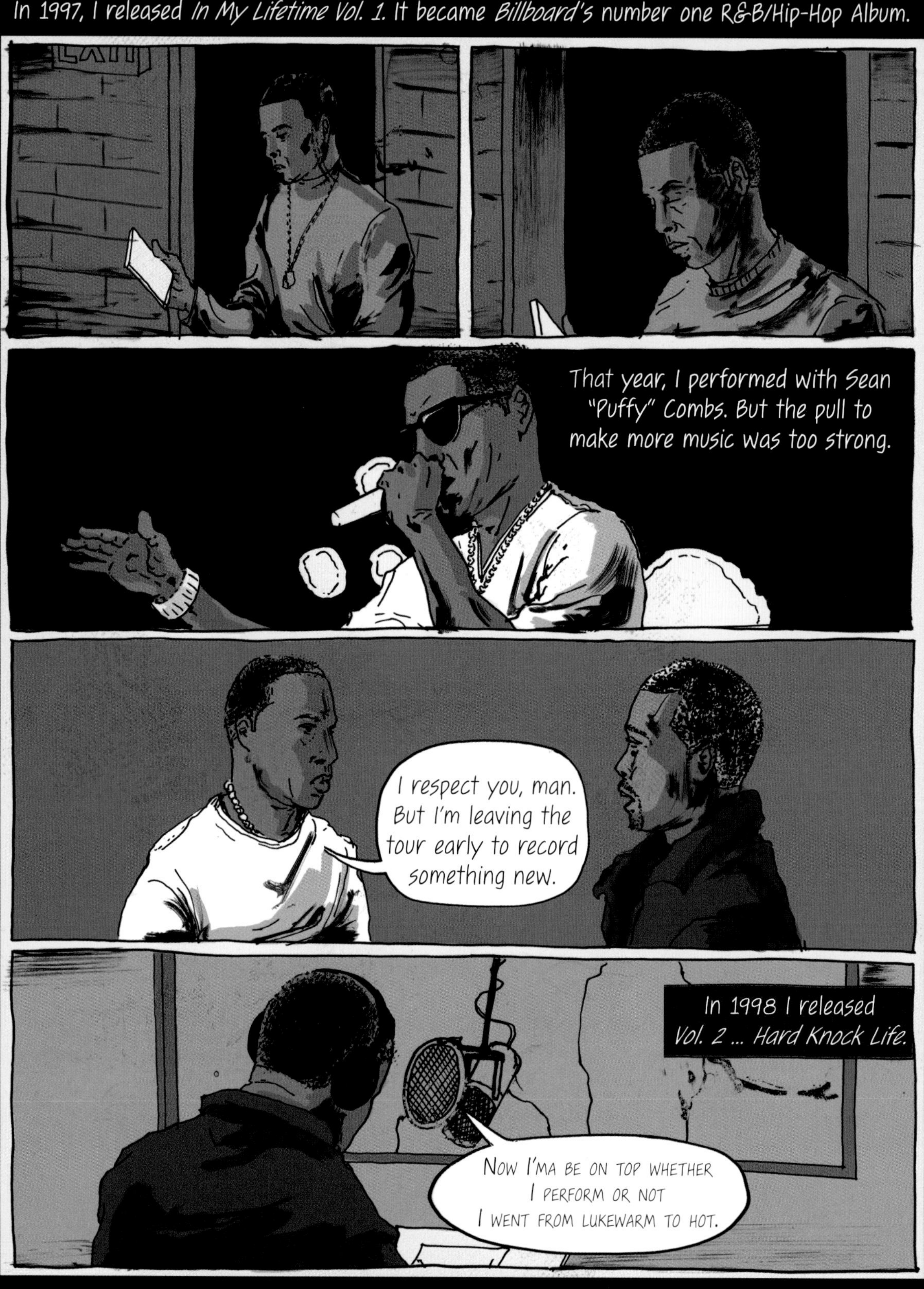
In 1997, I released *In My Lifetime Vol. 1.* It became *Billboard's* number one R&B/Hip-Hop Album.
That year, I performed with Sean "Puffy" Combs. But the pull to make more music was too strong.
I respect you, man. But I'm leaving the tour early to record something new.
In 1998 I released *Vol. 2 ... Hard Knock Life.*
NOW I'MA BE ON TOP WHETHER I PERFORM OR NOT I WENT FROM LUKEWARM TO HOT.

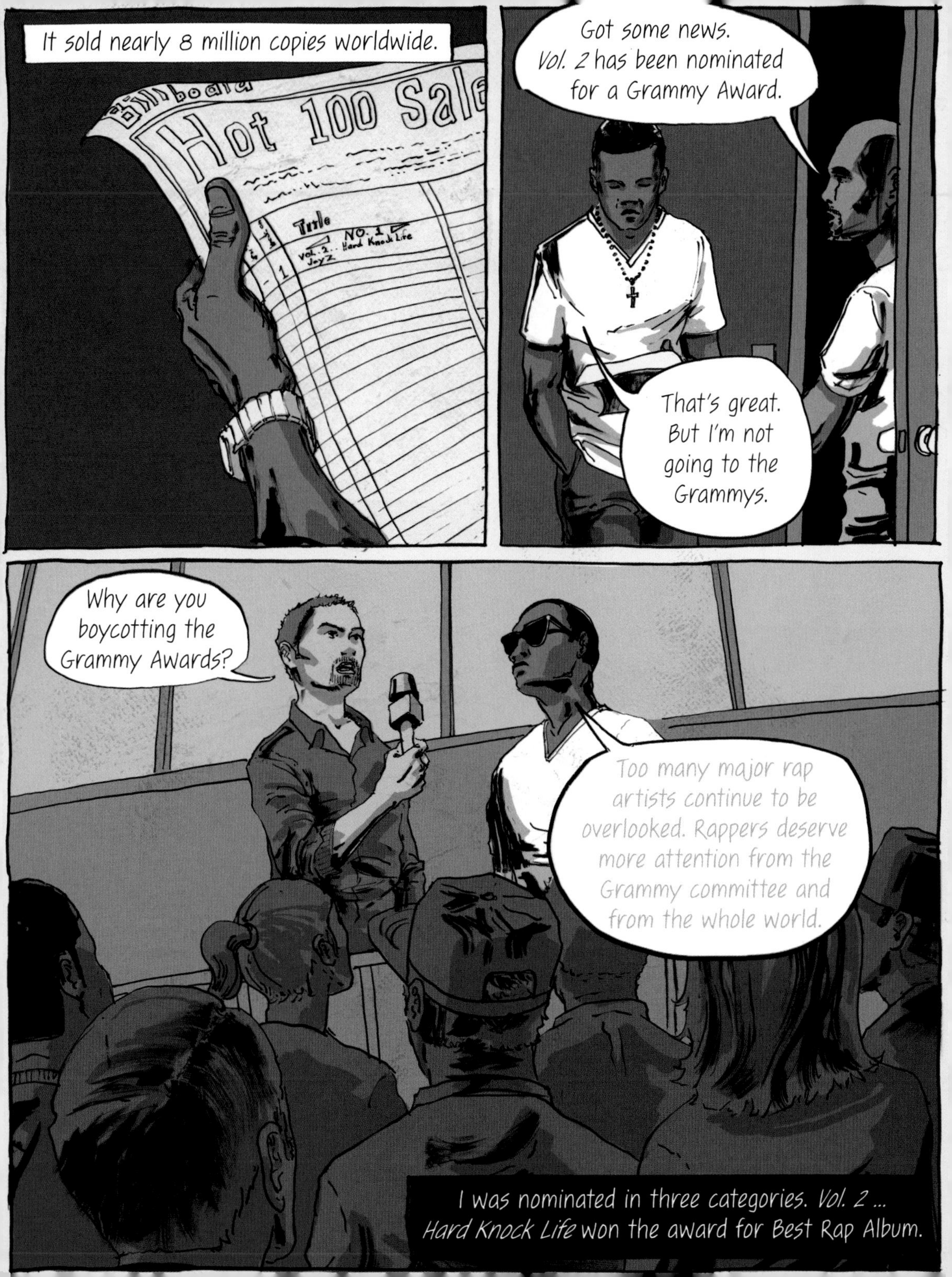
It sold nearly 8 million copies worldwide.
Billboard Hot 100 Sale
Title
NO. 1
Vol. 2... Hard Knock Life
Jay Z
Got some news. Vol. 2 has been nominated for a Grammy Award.
That's great. But I'm not going to the Grammys.
Why are you boycotting the Grammy Awards?
Too many major rap artists continue to be overlooked. Rappers deserve more attention from the Grammy committee and from the whole world.
I was nominated in three categories. Vol. 2 ... Hard Knock Life won the award for Best Rap Album.

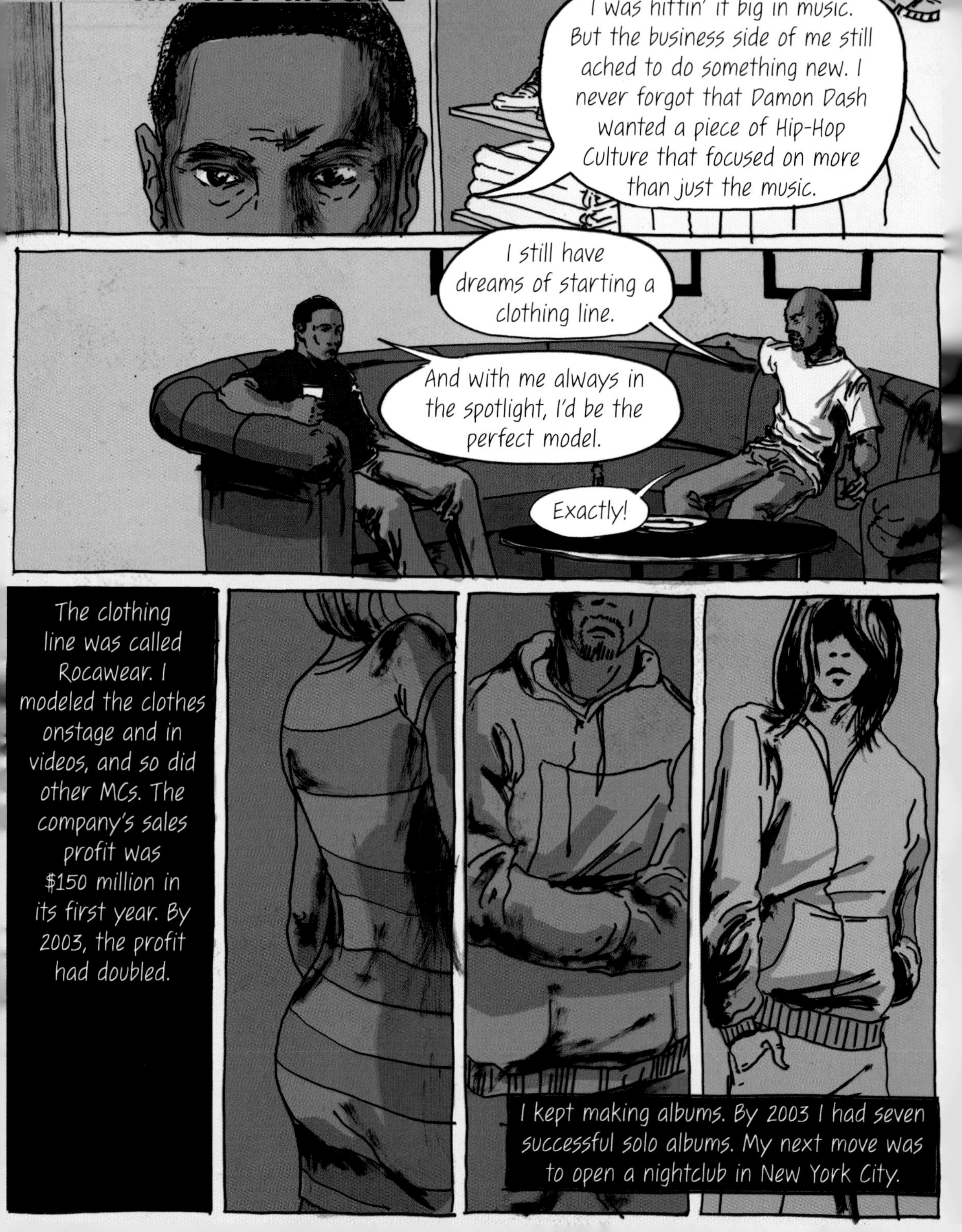
I was hittin' it big in music. But the business side of me still ached to do something new. I never forgot that Damon Dash wanted a piece of Hip-Hop Culture that focused on more than just the music.
I still have dreams of starting a clothing line.
And with me always in the spotlight, I'd be the perfect model.
Exactly!
The clothing line was called Rocawear. I modeled the clothes onstage and in videos, and so did other MCs. The company's sales profit was $150 million in its first year. By 2003, the profit had doubled.
I kept making albums. By 2003 I had seven successful solo albums. My next move was to open a nightclub in New York City.

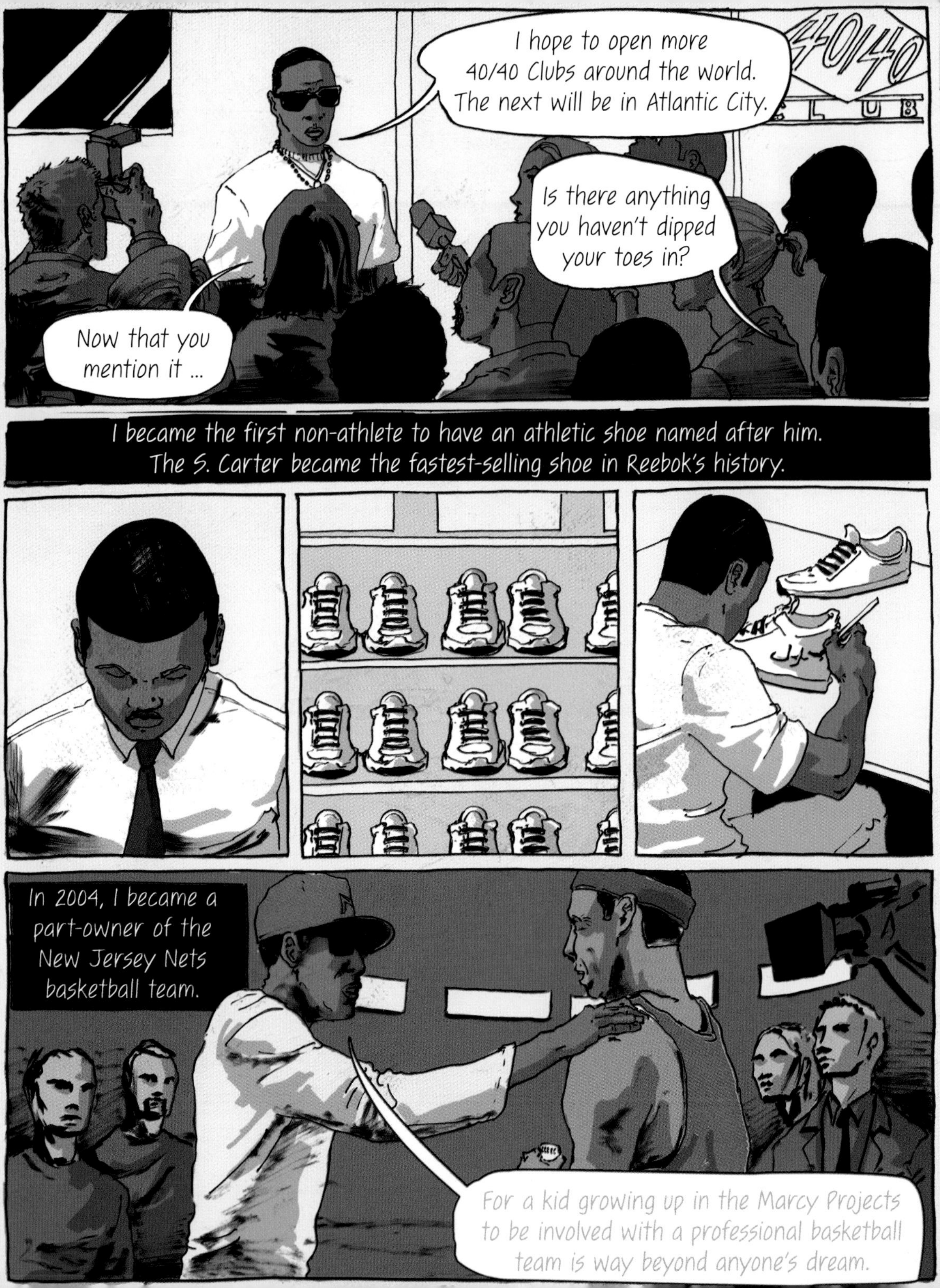

I hope to open more 40/40 Clubs around the world. The next will be in Atlantic City.
Is there anything you haven't dipped your toes in?
Now that you mention it ...
I became the first non-athlete to have an athletic shoe named after him. The S. Carter became the fastest-selling shoe in Reebok's history.
In 2004, I became a part-owner of the New Jersey Nets basketball team.
For a kid growing up in the Marcy Projects to be involved with a professional basketball team is way beyond anyone's dream.

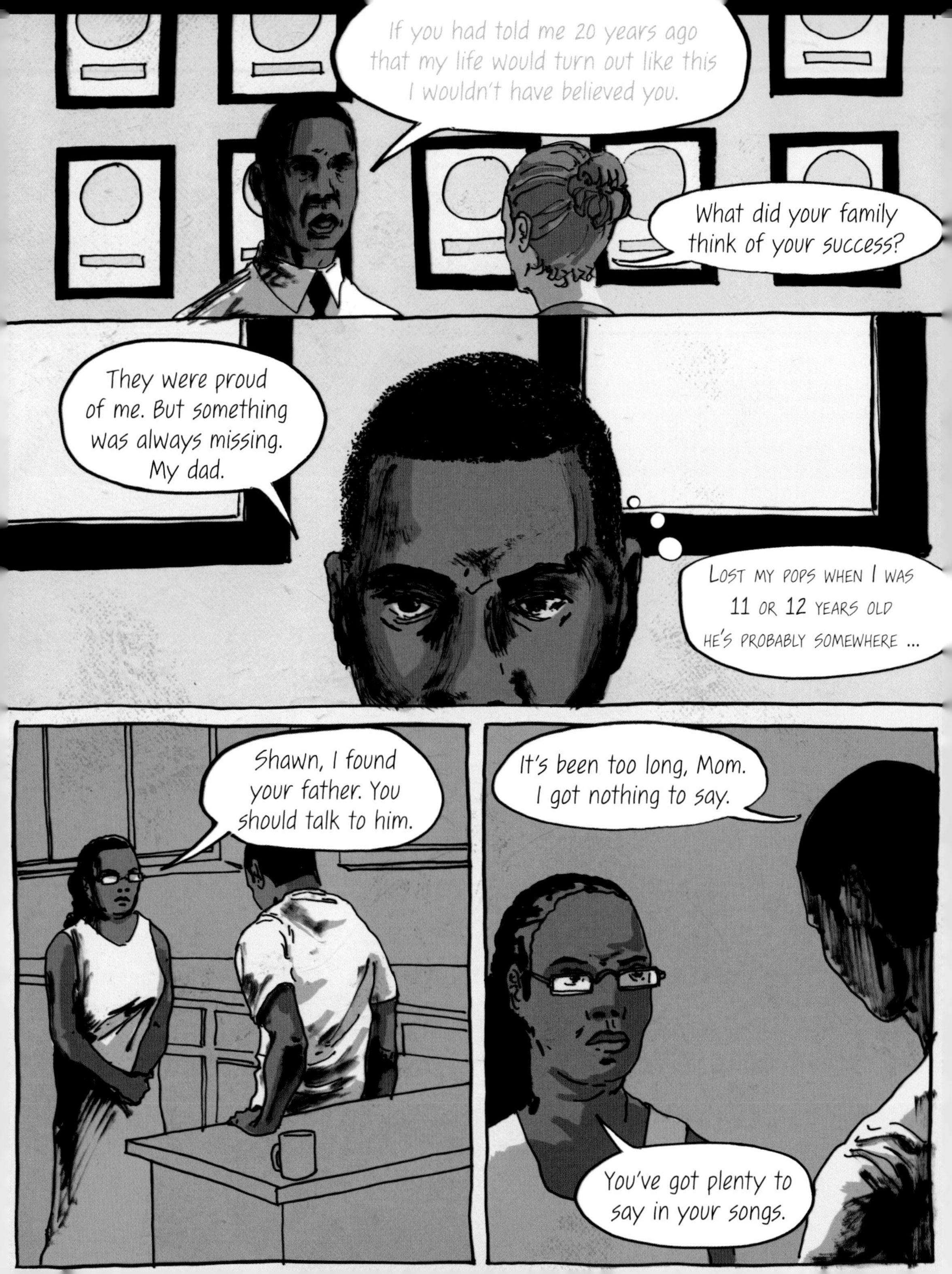
If you had told me 20 years ago that my life would turn out like this I wouldn't have believed you.
What did your family think of your success?
They were proud of me. But something was always missing. My dad.
LOST MY POPS WHEN I WAS 11 OR 12 YEARS OLD HE'S PROBABLY SOMEWHERE ...
Shawn, I found your father. You should talk to him.
It's been too long, Mom. I got nothing to say.
You've got plenty to say in your songs.

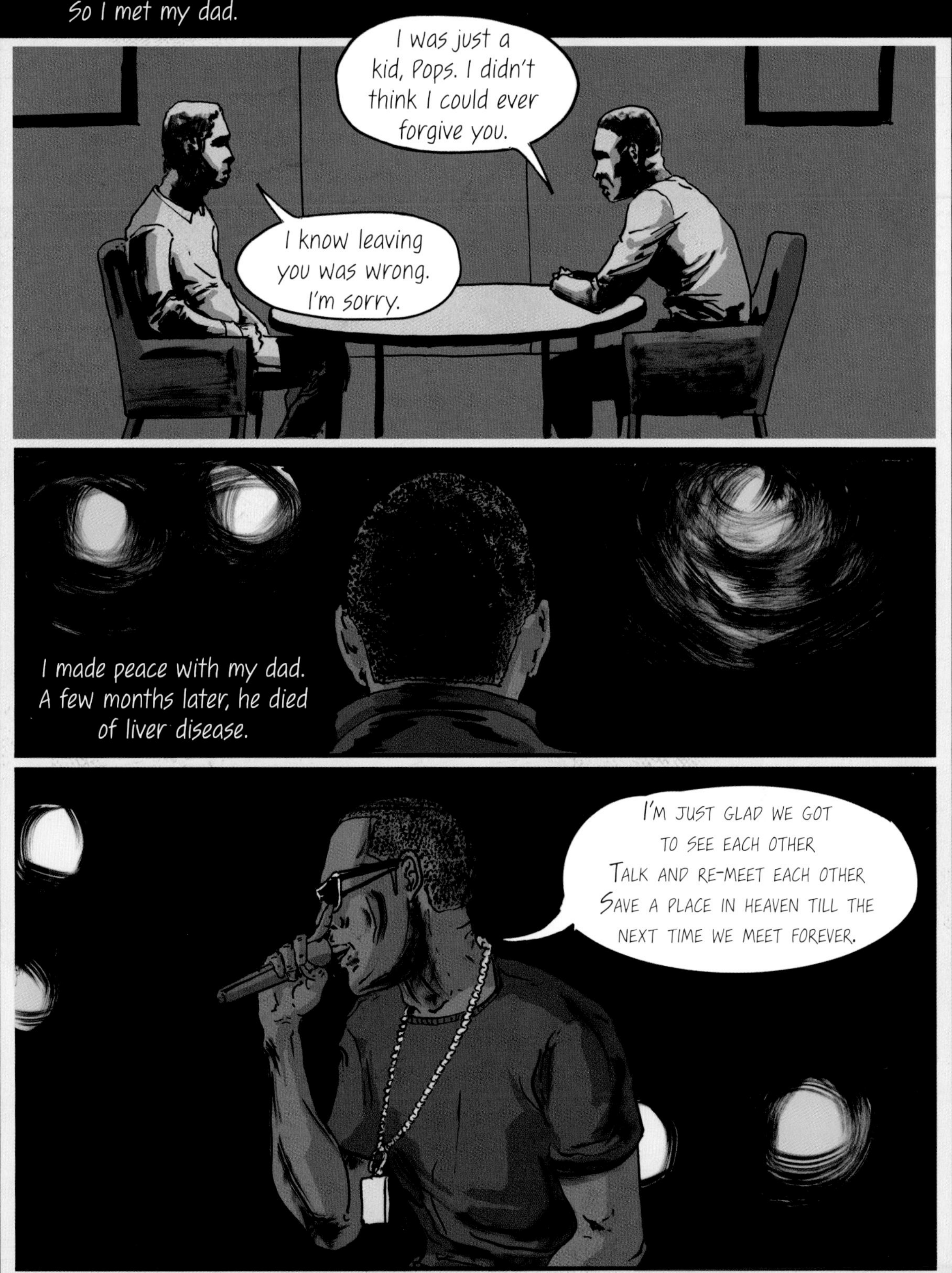
So I met my dad.
I was just a kid, Pops. I didn't think I could ever forgive you.
I know leaving you was wrong. I'm sorry.
I made peace with my dad. A few months later, he died of liver disease.
I'M JUST GLAD WE GOT TO SEE EACH OTHER
TALK AND RE-MEET EACH OTHER
SAVE A PLACE IN HEAVEN TILL THE NEXT TIME WE MEET FOREVER.

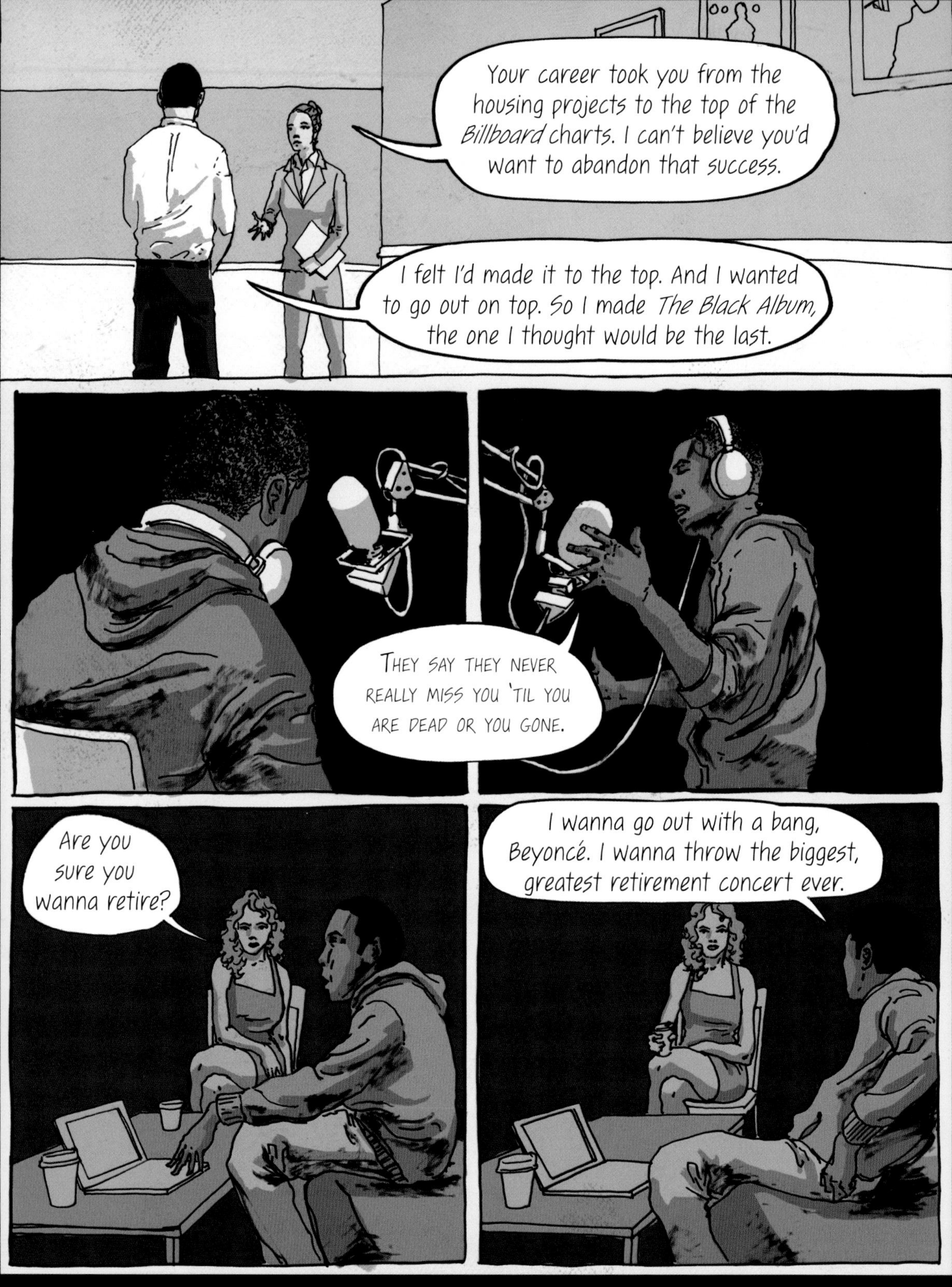
Your career took you from the housing projects to the top of the *Billboard* charts. I can't believe you'd want to abandon that success.
I felt I'd made it to the top. And I wanted to go out on top. So I made *The Black Album,* the one I thought would be the last.
THEY SAY THEY NEVER REALLY MISS YOU 'TIL YOU ARE DEAD OR YOU GONE.
Are you sure you wanna retire?
I wanna go out with a bang, Beyoncé. I wanna throw the biggest, greatest retirement concert ever.

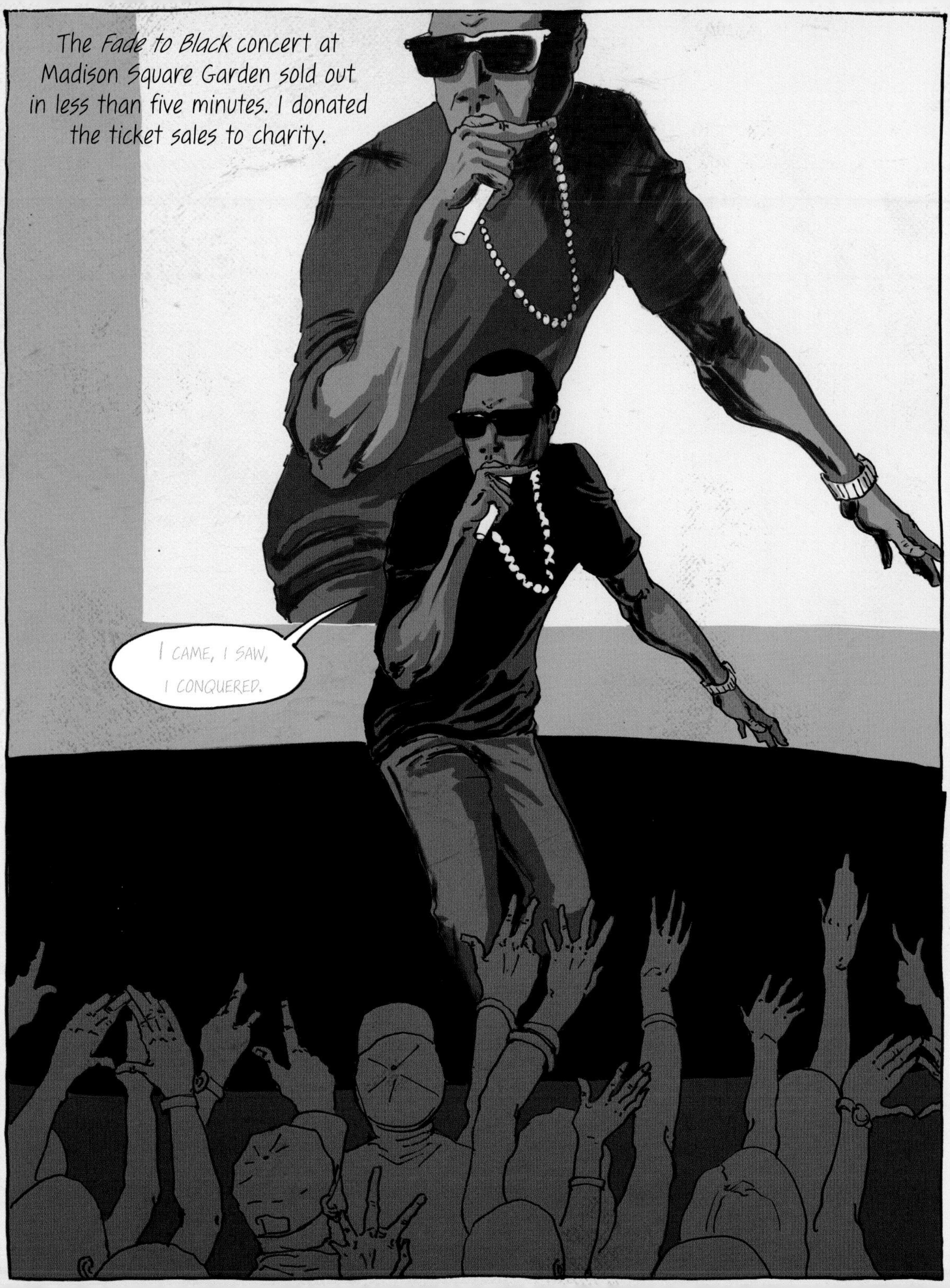
The *Fade to Black* concert at Madison Square Garden sold out in less than five minutes. I donated the ticket sales to charity.
I CAME, I SAW, I CONQUERED.

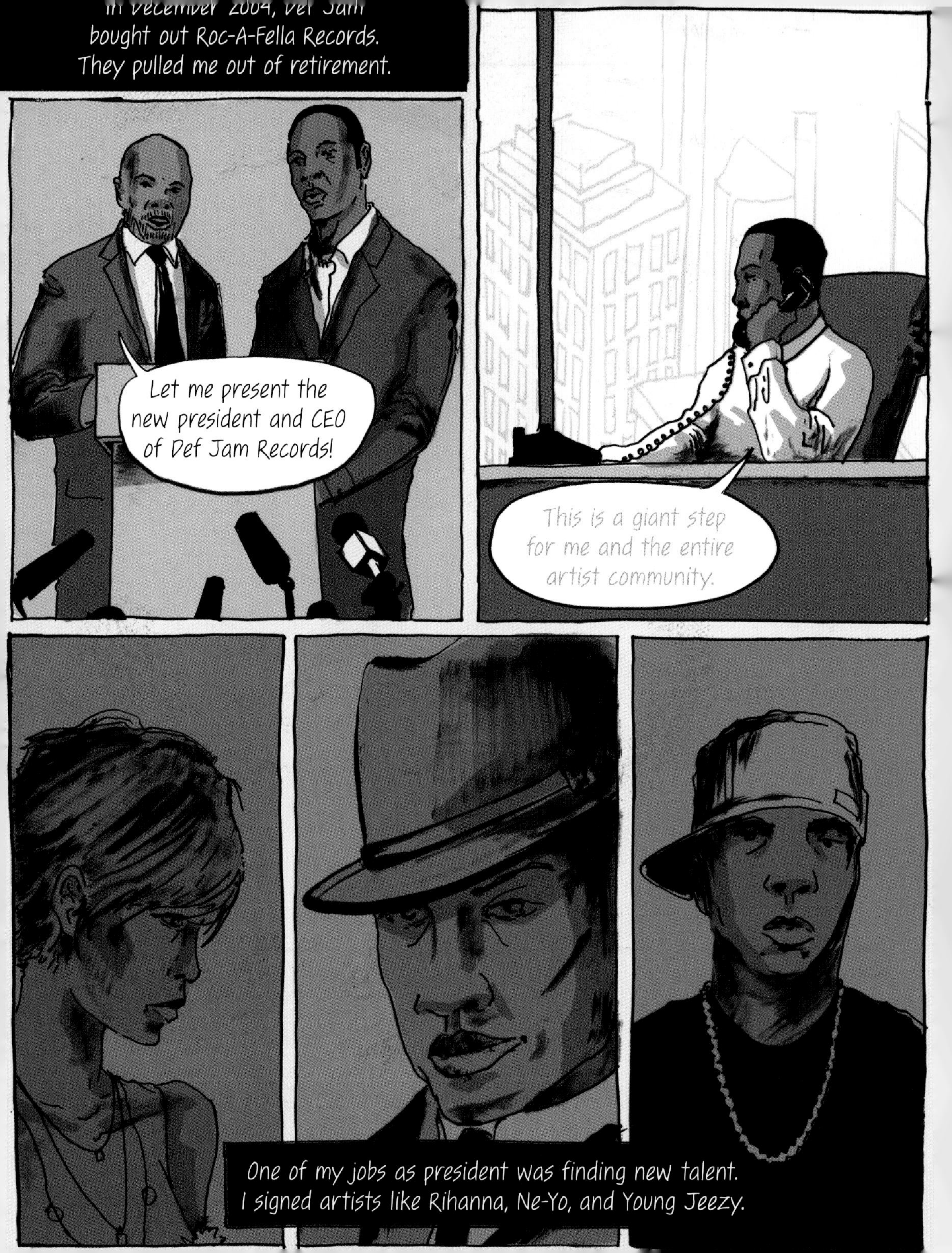
In December 2004, Def Jam bought out Roc-A-Fella Records. They pulled me out of retirement.
Let me present the new president and CEO of Def Jam Records!
This is a giant step for me and the entire artist community.
One of my jobs as president was finding new talent. I signed artists like Rihanna, Ne-Yo, and Young Jeezy.

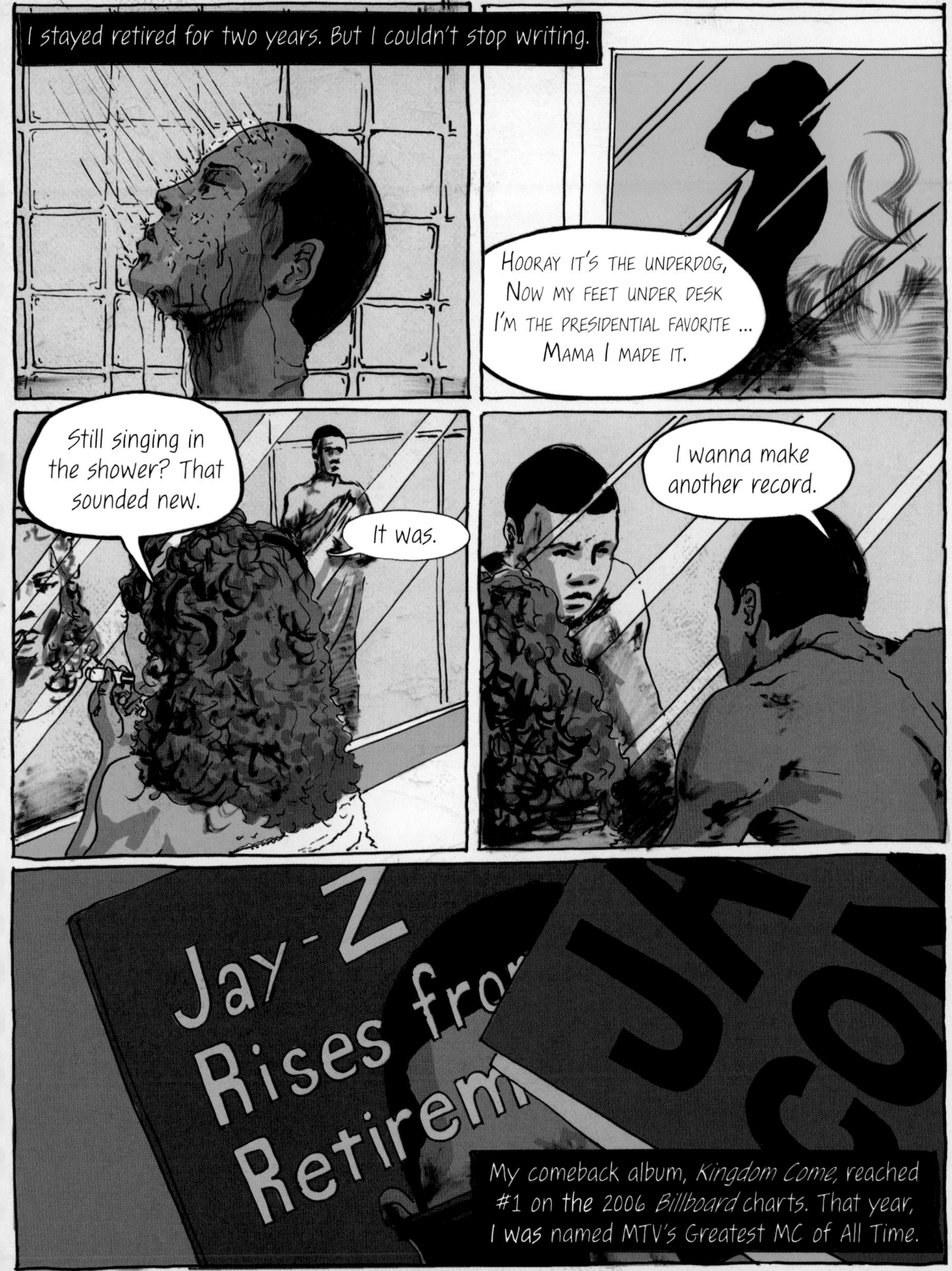
I stayed retired for two years. But I couldn't stop writing.
HOORAY IT'S THE UNDERDOG, NOW MY FEET UNDER DESK I'M THE PRESIDENTIAL FAVORITE ... MAMA I MADE IT.
Still singing in the shower? That sounded new.
It was.
I wanna make another record.
Jay-Z Rises from Retirem
My comeback album, Kingdom Come, reached #1 on the 2006 Billboard charts. That year, I was named MTV's Greatest MC of All Time.

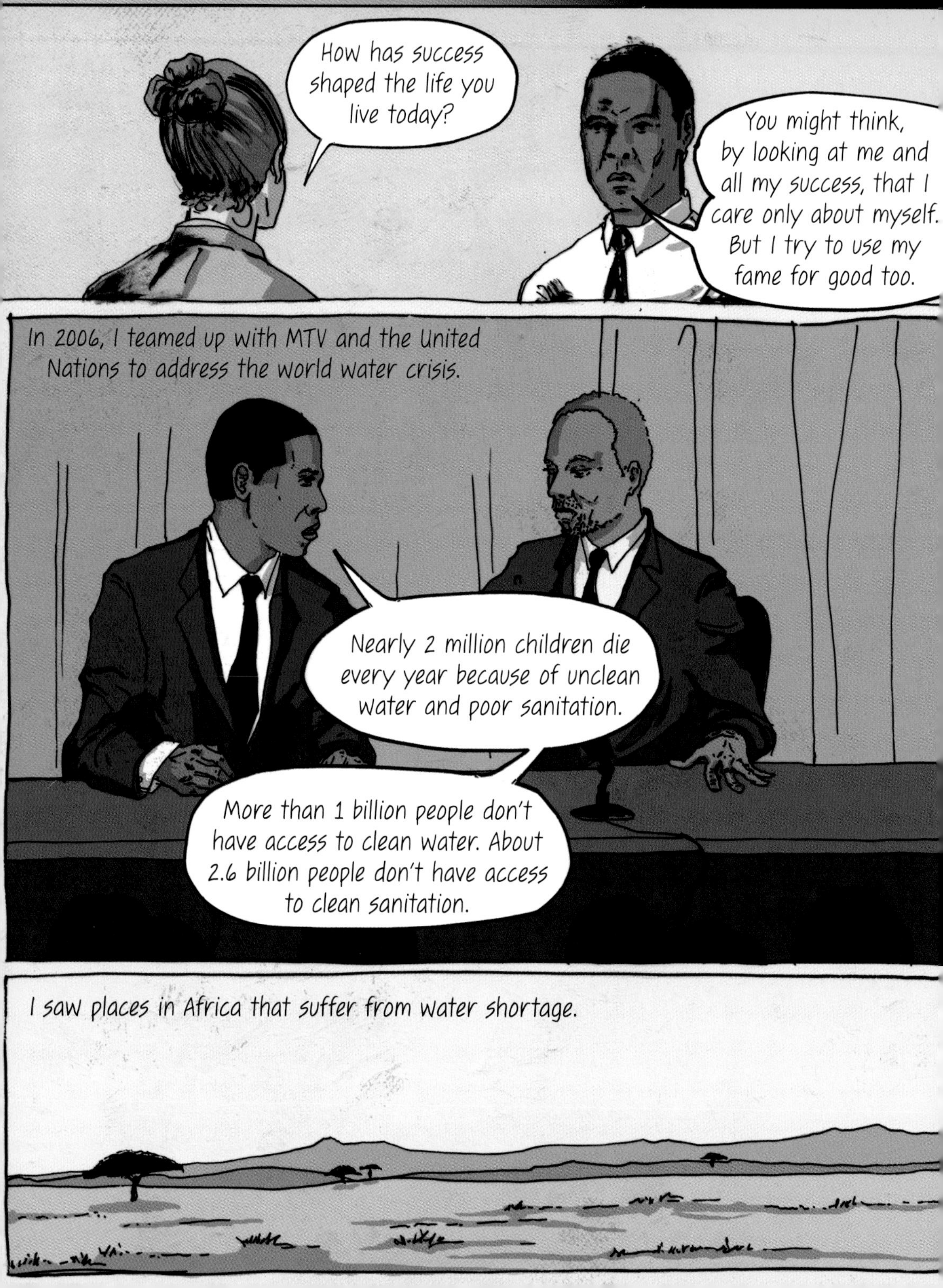
How has success shaped the life you live today?
You might think, by looking at me and all my success, that I care only about myself. But I try to use my fame for good too.
In 2006, I teamed up with MTV and the United Nations to address the world water crisis.
Nearly 2 million children die every year because of unclean water and poor sanitation.
More than 1 billion people don't have access to clean water. About 2.6 billion people don't have access to clean sanitation.
I saw places in Africa that suffer from water shortage.

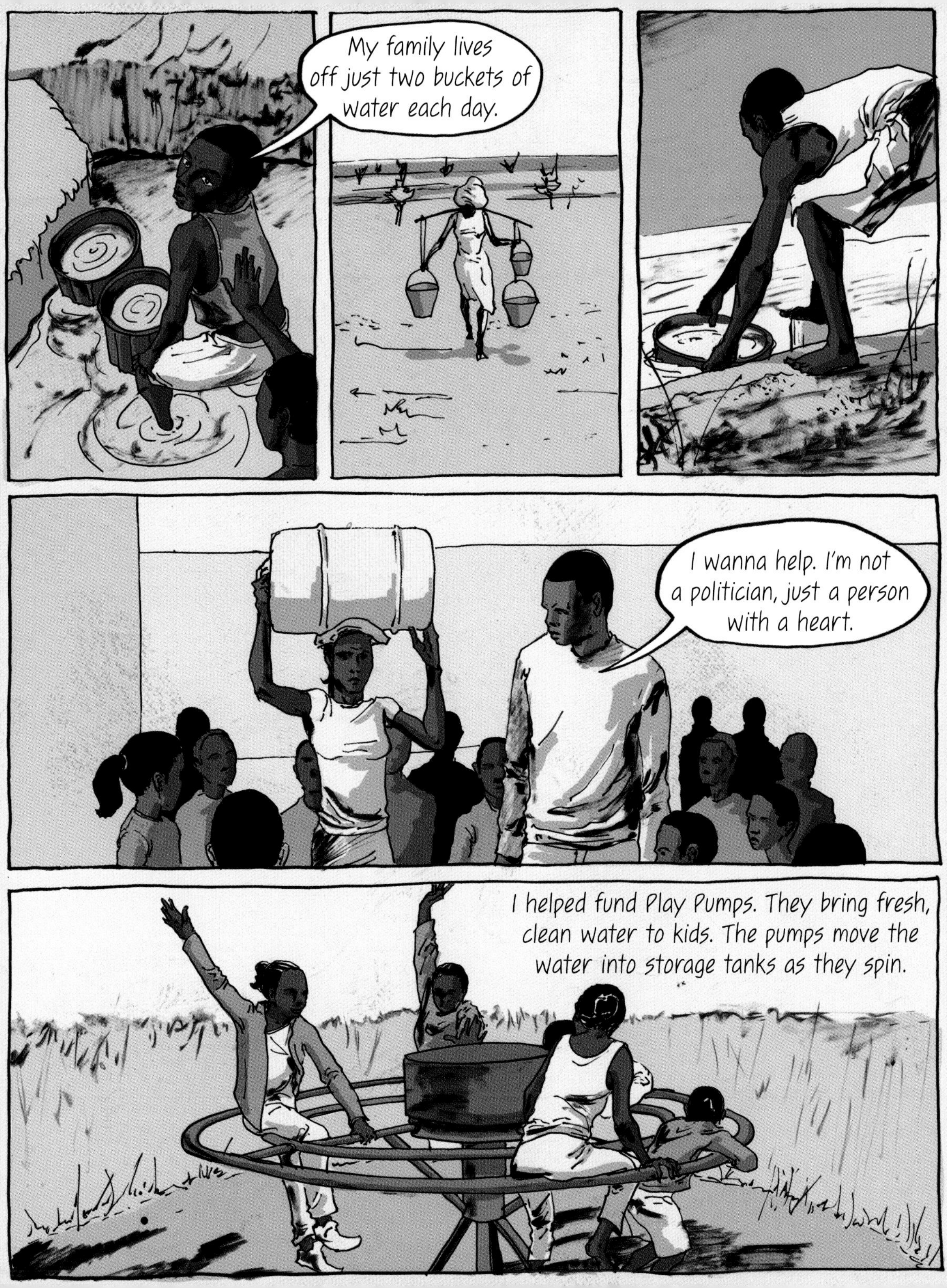

My family lives off just two buckets of water each day.
I wanna help. I'm not a politician, just a person with a heart.
I helped fund Play Pumps. They bring fresh, clean water to kids. The pumps move the water into storage tanks as they spin.

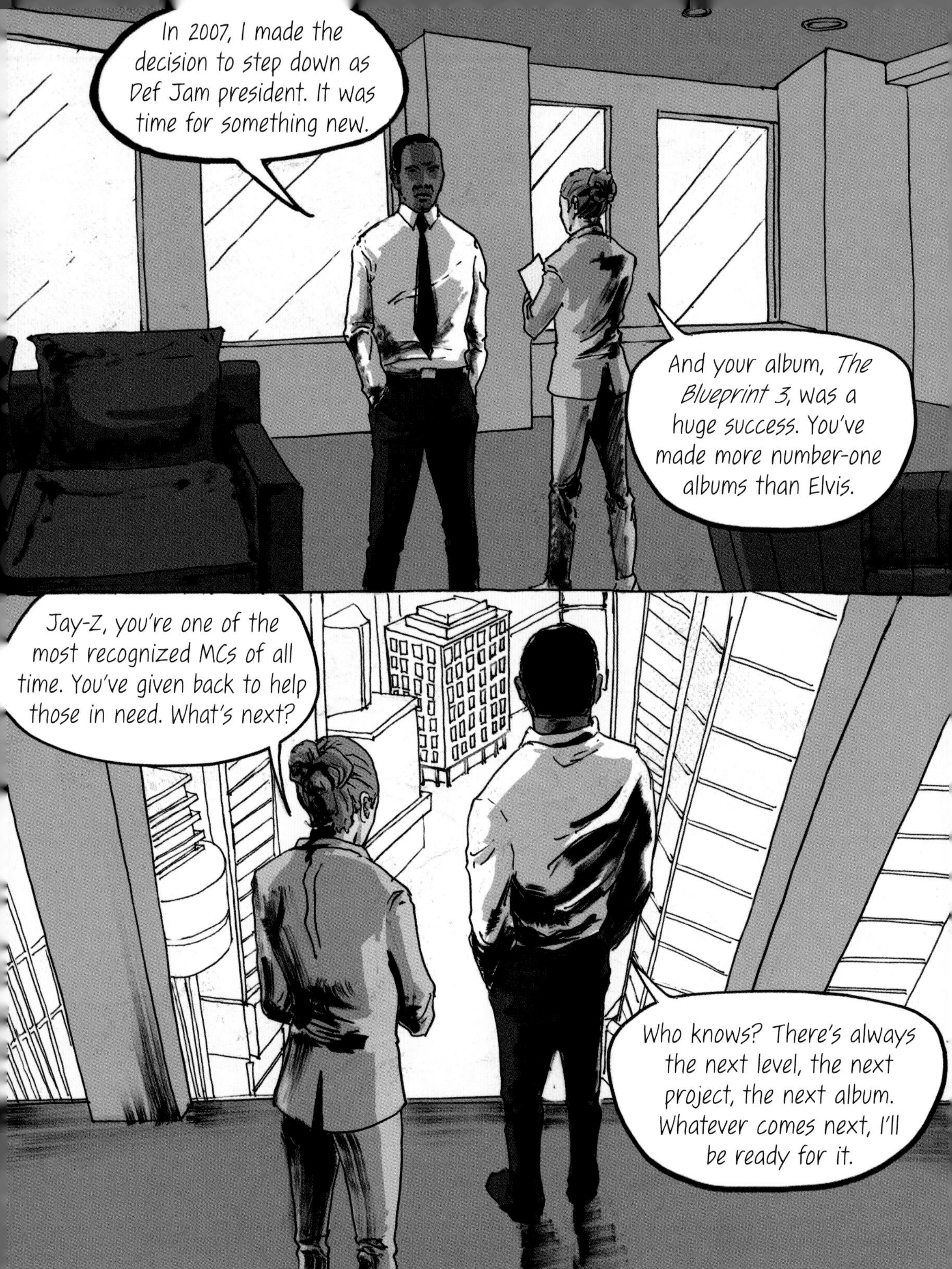
In 2007, I made the decision to step down as Def Jam president. It was time for something new.
And your album, *The Blueprint 3*, was a huge success. You've made more number-one albums than Elvis.
Jay-Z, you're one of the most recognized MCs of all time. You've given back to help those in need. What's next?
Who knows? There's always the next level, the next project, the next album. Whatever comes next, I'll be ready for it.

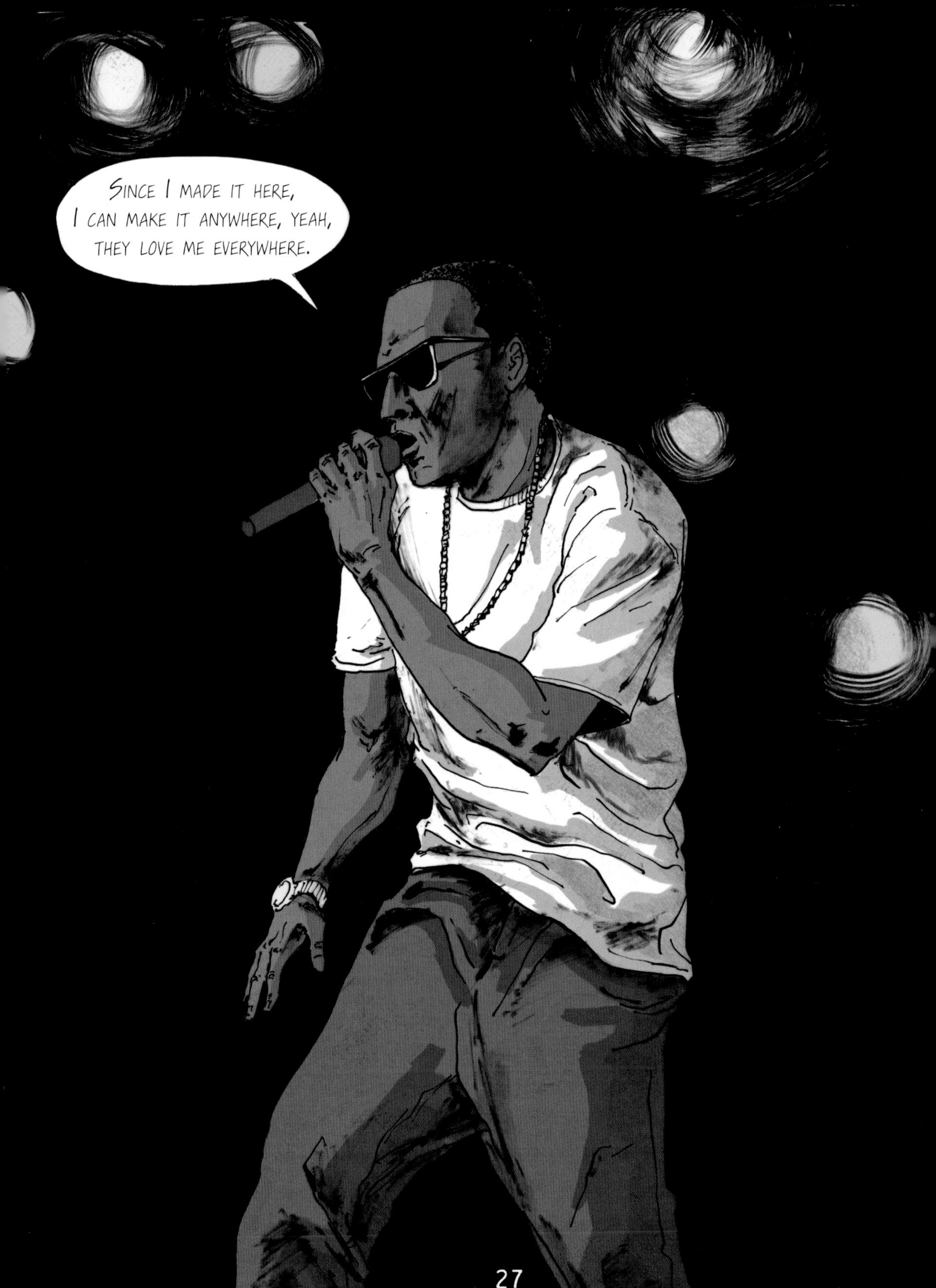
SINCE I MADE IT HERE, I CAN MAKE IT ANYWHERE, YEAH, THEY LOVE ME EVERYWHERE.

AN MC FROM BROOKLYN

JAY-Z grew up in the Marcy Houses projects in Brooklyn, New York. Residents often heard gunfire and saw fights. When he was nine years old, Jay-Z witnessed a murder. At age 12, he was shot. Jay-Z said he felt worthless as a child. "People would get shot, people would get killed, and it would never be in the paper or on the news or anything," he said. "So we were like, 'our lives ain't even worth reporting.'" But he doesn't regret his life experiences. In fact, his experiences have made him even **MORE GRATEFUL** for the things he has.

Jay-Z's songs are often personal. They tell of his life as a kid growing up in the projects, his relationships, and his struggles in the music world. His gritty lyrics, innovative beats, and high sales earned him the nickname of "King of Rap." He is known for his talent as an MC, rapping and rhyming skillfully to a beat. In 2009, MTV named him one of the top five MCs of all time. Rob Sheffield of *Rolling Stone* magazine called him the "Michelangelo of flow" and **"A TRUE ORIGINAL FROM DAY ONE."**

Although some critics and rap artists have accused Jay-Z of being too commercial, his musical ability is what draws a **VARIETY OF LISTENERS.** He has collaborated with groups such as Linkin Park, Coldplay, and the White Stripes. In 2008, Jay-Z became the first hip-hop artist to headline the Glastonbury Festival. This rock festival is held in England. That year, he also married his longtime girlfriend, Beyoncé Knowles.

Jay-Z has become not only a successful hip-hop artist and pop culture icon, but also a business mogul. His many business ventures have increased his fortune, and in 2009 he was named one of the 20 wealthiest black Americans by *Forbes* magazine. As Jay-Z once rapped, **"I'M NOT A BUSINESSMAN, I'M A BUSINESS, MAN."**

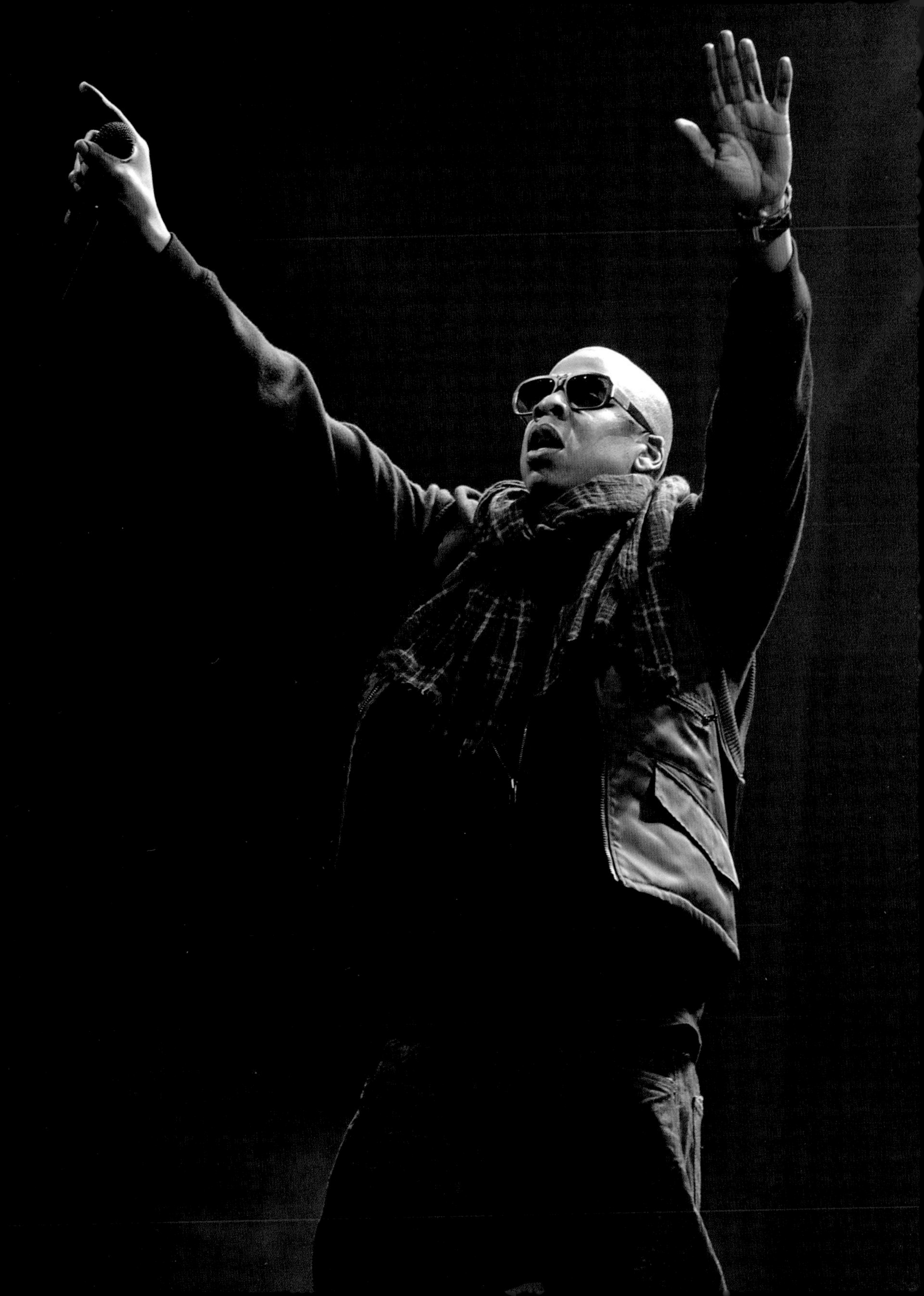

GLOSSARY

DJ (DEE-jay)—Disc Jockey; DJs play pre-precorded music for a radio, party, or club audience

empire (EM-pire)—a large group of companies controlled by one person

executive (ig-ZE-kyuh-tiv)—a person who holds a senior position in a company and is involved in planning its future

Hip-Hop Culture (HIP HOP KUHL-chuhr)—a form of social expression that revolves around graffiti, DJs, breakdancing, and MCs

MC (em-SEE)—Master of Ceremonies; MCs rap and rhyme to beats played by a DJ

mogul (MO-guhl)—a very powerful person

nominate (NOM-uh-nate)—name someone as a candidate for an award

record label (REK-urd LAY-buhl)—a company that manages the brand and trademark used to market music; the record label produces, promotes, and distributes the music to the public

sanitation (san-uh-TAY-shuhn)—systems for cleaning the water supply and disposing of sewage

venture (VEN-shuhr)—a project that is somewhat risky

READ MORE

Abrams, Dennis. *Jay-Z.* Hip-Hop Stars. New York: Chelsea House, 2008.

Garofoli, Wendy. *Hip-Hop History.* Hip-Hop World. Mankato, Minn.: Capstone Press, 2010.

Heos, Bridget. *Jay-Z.* Library of Hip-Hop Biographies. New York: Rosen Publishing, 2009.

INTERNET

FactHound offers a safe, fun way to find Internet sites related to this book. All of the sites on FactHound have been researched by our staff.

Here's all you do:

Visit *www.facthound.com*

Type in this code: 9781429660174

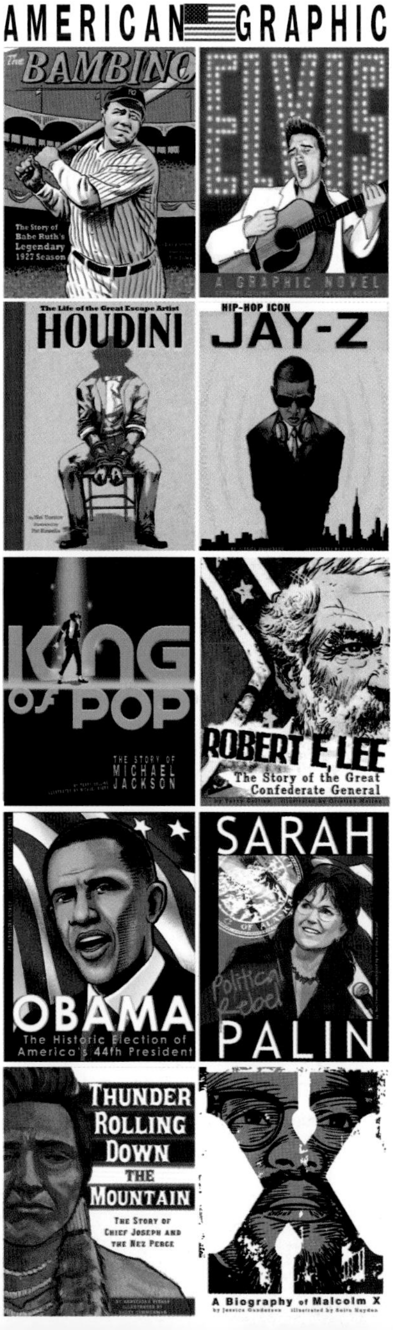
AMERICAN GRAPHIC
The BAMBINO
The Story of Babe Ruth's Legendary 1927 Season
ELVIS
A GRAPHIC NOVEL
The Life of the Great Escape Artist
HOUDINI
HIP-HOP ICON
JAY-Z
KING OF POP
THE STORY OF MICHAEL JACKSON
ROBERT E. LEE
The Story of the Great Confederate General
OBAMA
The Historic Election of America's 44th President
SARAH
Political Rebel
PALIN
THUNDER ROLLING DOWN THE MOUNTAIN
THE STORY OF CHIEF JOSEPH AND THE NEZ PERCE
X
A Biography of Malcolm X

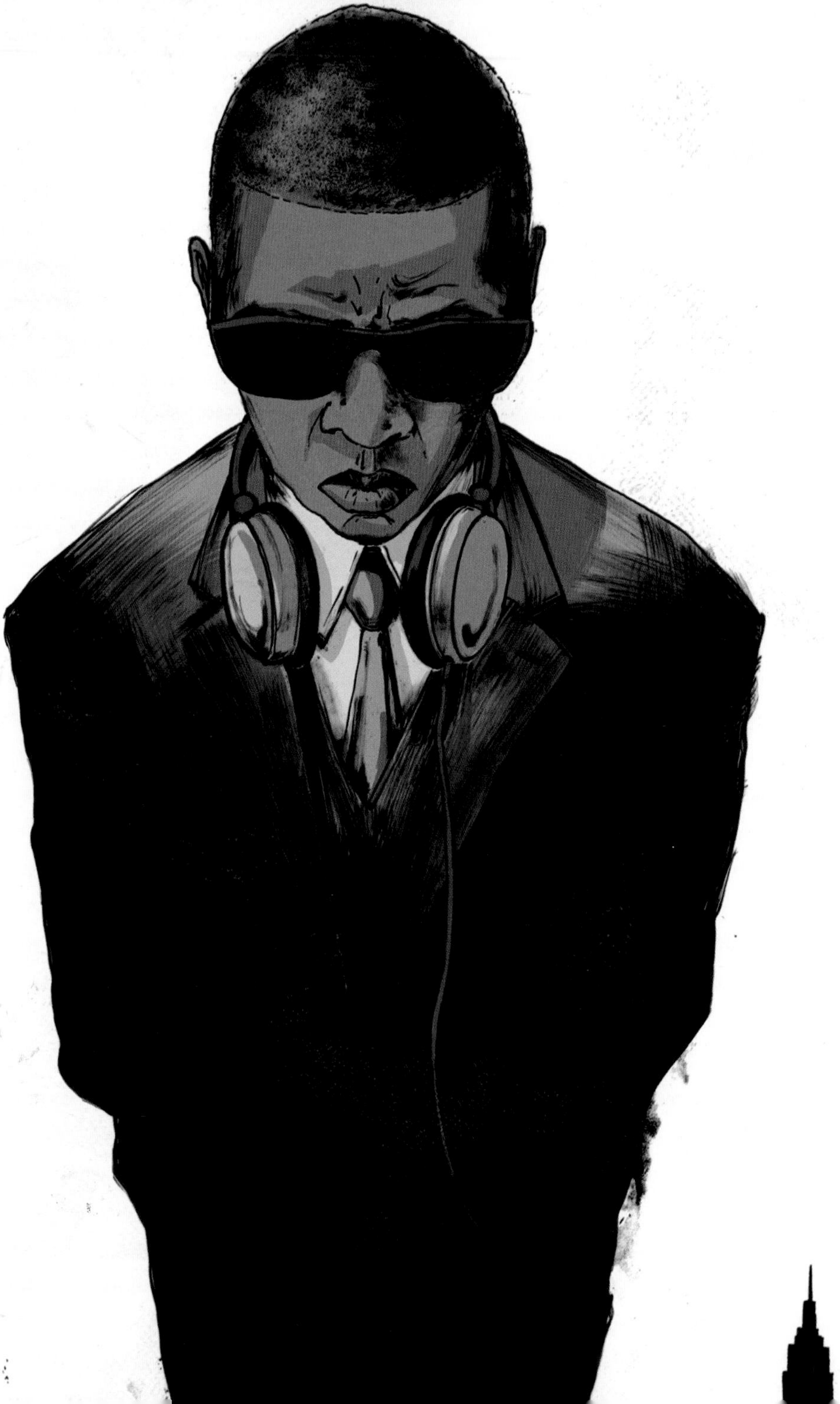